At 50, Your Warranty Expires
and everything falls apart

© 2005 Thomas Dryden
All Rights Reserved.

No part of this publication may be reproduced, stored in a retrieval system, or transmitted, in any form or by any means, electronic, mechanical, photocopying, recording, or otherwise, without the written permission of the author.

First published by Dog Ear Publishing
4010 W. 86th Street, Ste H
Indianapolis, IN 46268
www.dogearpublishing.net

dog ear
PUBLISHING

ISBN: 1-59858-048-5

This book is printed on acid-free paper.

Printed in the United States of America

At 50, Your Warranty Expires and everything falls apart

Tom Dryden

Contents

Introduction	1
Tommy can you hear me	7
Joe Valentine	11
I'll gladly pay you tomorrow	14
Hawkin' to my generation	18
Life is too short to eat fruit	21
Fantasyland	25
AARPing up the wrong tree	29
End-user experiences	32
Alice doesn't eat here any more	36
The crude truth	40
Ol' Blue Eyes is back	43
You've got mail (not to mention an amazing Venus)	47
A night at the Molokai	50
Prisoners of love	54
Hometown banking with the personal touch	57
No place to go but up	60
A song of myselves	63
A little less conversation	67
The Tin Man was on to something	70
The Wurlitzer inside my head	73
The boy who made change	76
Uncle Henry would agree	79
The Belgian blockhead	83
Bonnie, Clyde and the art of Feng Shui	87
Our menu options have changed	91
A letter from Santa	95

A little romance..99
Velma Rae and her silver polishing pads................102
The cable guy...105
Cheyenne, my commie banker.................................109
Stranger in a strange land...113
So where's Suzanne Pleshette..................................116
Your airline of choice...119
It's that least wonderful time....................................124
Daniel Boone would disown me..............................128
Charlton Heston drops in...131
New Jersey's next Poet Laureate..............................135
Harassment 101..138
I brake for bumper stickers......................................141
How to succeed in business.....................................144
Seems like a fair trade to me....................................148
While you were sleeping..151
'Till we meet again. And again. And again...............155
Saturday at the mall..158
Many happy returns..161
Plastic surgery gone awry..165
The divine Honest Abe..168
A double date with Trista and Ryan........................172
A shorts story...175
Parents' weekend..178
You have 14 messages...182
Trust in the Lard...185
A day by the bay..189
How I'll spend eternity..192
Hogging the phone...195
How about a martini...199
A career change..202
A bimbette's story...206

To Judy

Introduction

The summer of my 47th year I treated myself to something I had always wanted—a BMW 3-series convertible.

I ordered it from a dealer near my Connecticut home and arranged to take delivery at the factory in Germany.

I picked up the car on a Monday morning and, over the next 24 hours before I dropped it off at the Munich airport, blew through southern Germany, western Austria, the Tyrolean Alps of Italy, eastern Switzerland and all of Liechtenstein at speeds of up to 130 mph. BMW shipped it to the U.S., where it arrived a month later.

It is said you should never love something that can't love you back, but I genuinely loved my silver-metallic baby with its gray leather upholstery. Every time I sat behind the wheel I was reminded of our honeymoon during which we got to know each other intimately, navigating the high speed autobahns and twisty Alpine roads the car was engineered to handle.

I drove it happily for four trouble-free years, watching with dread the odometer creep toward the 50,000 mile mark at which the warranty would expire.

The day that happened, I was barreling down I-95 at 80 mph. With the odometer displaying 49,999.9 miles, the "Check Engine" light came on.

I couldn't have brought the car to a stop before it hit the big 5-0 if I tried.

The dealer's service people never could figure out why the light came on a few yards shy of the 50,000-mile mark, and why, despite resetting it a dozen times, it stayed on for the next two years as slowly but surely the automotive love-of-my-life became sluggish and developed bizarre afflictions. They claimed it was a coincidence.

Nobody will ever convince me the manufacturer hadn't programmed it into the car at the factory, because the same thing happened when I hit 50.

One day I was 49 years and 364 days old and everything was running smoothly.

The next day it wasn't.

To wit, the day before my fiftieth birthday, I could hear a pin drop in another state.

Now I have to keep the TV turned up full blast.

My wife complains about the noise, so I rarely watch any more. I read instead.

But I've had to buy reading glasses, which I can never find because I have trouble remembering where I left them the night before.

My memory is becoming selective. I can recall November 22, 1963, like it was yesterday, but I sometimes have trouble remembering what I asked employees of my ad agency to do five minutes ago.

The teeth on one side of my mouth have become hyper-sensitive to cold or heat because, according to the dentist, my gums are receding.

Within a week of 50, I noticed that I was sprouting honest-to-God boobs. So I joined a gym to firm up and kept at it faithfully for three years. Last time I went, I was able to do 53 chin-ups—one for each year.

The next morning I woke up with tendonitis in both shoulders, along with a pinched nerve in the neck that made it impossible to hold my head erect.

Doctors told me I should stop working out, leaving me with two options: 1. Disregard them and continue going to the gym. My chest will be firm and manly but I'll have to learn to live with stabbing shoulder pain and a head that swivels uncontrollably like Linda Blair's in *The Exorcist*. 2. Stop lifting weights, live pain-free and wear a C cup.

Some choice.

For my first 50 years, I was able to eat whatever I wanted. Not any more.

At 50, my cholesterol level skyrocketed and I had to start taking Lipitor and restricting my diet.

At 49, I made do with one chin. But now I'm developing a second. Gravity, you know.

And my hair's thinning at the temples. Just a bit mind you, but I can see some scalp. The good news: I have a new hair. The bad news: It's sprouting out of my left ear. I've cut it. I've tweezed it. It keeps growing back, thicker and longer than before.

Pluck it.

A few days ago I was eating a peach at my desk. "You're making a mess," someone said, pointing to juice that had dribbled down my chin onto my shirt and keyboard, as I munched away, blissfully unaware that, forevermore, like the title character of T.S. Elliott's "Love Song of J. Alfred Prufrock," I will have to worry about daring to eat a peach in public.

Now I know what old T.S. was trying to say.

About the time I turned 50, I began to realize that the mantra my 92-old-mother has been repeating for years is true: Nothing makes sense any more.

There's simply no explanation for Americans continuing to drive gas-guzzling SUVs when we're completely dependent on oil imported from wacko Middle Eastern nations whose inhabitants want to kill us so they can go to paradise where they will be rewarded by being allowed to deflower 70 virgins. (Better bring along plenty of Cialis, guys.)

Nor is there any way to explain how companies like Enron and WorldCom were able for years to report billions in profits when, in fact, they earned less money than I am carrying in my wallet this very minute. You would think that someone in the accounts payable department might have noticed the checkbook was short a couple of billion dollars or so, but nobody did. Maybe they were so busy attending management training workshops they didn't have time to ask questions.

It's impossible to explain why Hollywood executives continue to allow Adam Sandler to make movies.

Or why O.J. is walking around, free as a bird.

Or why the mega-bank in which I have maintained a five-figure money market account for years—the same bank that's running TV spots touting how much it cares about its customers—just sent a letter announcing that, from now on, I'm expected to fork over $125 a year for the privilege of keeping my money on deposit.

I always thought it was supposed to be the other way around.

Silly me.

I recently sold the convertible, which was becoming ridiculously expensive to maintain, to a used car dealer who completely reconditioned it. Last time I drove by the dealer's lot, it had a "Like New" sign in its window.

I know better. That car has been around the block a million times. So have I, but I'm not complaining.

So what if my manufacturer has turned on my Check Engine light? A hundred years ago the life expectancy of the average American man was 46.2 years. If this were another time, I would have been dead nearly seven years.

My warranty may have expired, but at 53, I have lots of miles left in me. And those miles are sure to be the sweetest of all because of the many valuable lessons I've learned along the roads I've traveled.

I just wish I could remember some of them.

Tommy can you hear me?

"You wanna have another baby?" my wife asked out of the blue the other morning as we were eating breakfast.

"Are you insane? We'd be wearing Pampers by time the kid grew out of them," I replied.

"Watch my lips," she said, taking my chin in her hand and swiveling my head toward her face, like a fed-up mother does with an out-of-sorts child. "Do. You. Want. Half. My. Bagel?"

She mumbles. Always has, but she's been mumbling more than ever lately. So have my sons. And my employees. And the cast of *The Sopranos*. It's a conspiracy to make me think I'm losing my hearing. I most assuredly am not, though I will admit hearing loss runs in the family.

My grandma began losing her hearing in her forties. Her grandchildren still laugh about the time in the 1950s when my Aunt Betty, noticing the porch of her house was rotting, called a home termite inspector. Several days later when the doorbell rang, my aunt was on the phone, so she asked grandma to get the door.

After a few minutes, grandma walked back into the kitchen. "Who was that, mama?" my aunt asked.

"It was some man who said he was a home permanent inspector. I told him we get ours done at the beauty shop."

The deafness gene passed on to my mother but it took a while—90 years—to show up. Two years ago my siblings and I started noticing we had to repeat things for mom, who adamantly denied there was anything wrong. Finally, my sister, who was taking mom to attend her daughter's Sarah Lawrence commencement at which Barbara Walters was to speak, talked our mother into going to an audiologist, and said she would accompany her.

Mom went, but not happily.

The audiologist asked, "Wouldn't you like to be able to hear what the preacher says on Sundays?"

"As a matter of fact I wouldn't," mom replied. "He's the most boring preacher on earth. It would be merciful if I didn't have to listen to him drone on and on."

The audiologist tried again. "Well then, I understand you're going to see Barbara Walters speak at your granddaughter's graduation. Wouldn't you like to be able to understand her?"

"Nobody can understand Barbara Walters. She needs speech therapy."

Mom finally relented after seeing the microscopic size of today's hearing aids. Still vain as a school girl, she had feared having to wear one of the large battery-operated contraptions her mother had worn.

The next day mom e-mailed her children. "I've found a hearing aid small enough that it fits into my ear canal so nobody can tell I'm wearing it, but it costs $3,000. It's your inheritance, should I spend that kind of money?"

We replied that she shouldn't—we were planning a sibling reunion in Vegas and needed that cash for the craps table. She ordered it anyway, as we hoped she would.

Several weeks later at the graduation ceremony as Babwa Wawa was talking, mom defiantly removed the hearing aid and made a show of putting it in her purse. "I can hear her just fine," she announced. "And I'm right. She doesn't speak plainly."

For the last few years, my family has been nagging me to get my hearing tested.

I had no intention of doing so—it isn't my fault they mumble—until New Year's Eve, when my wife and I went to a black-tie dinner where we shared a table with another couple. The wife, I noticed, was wearing lots of make-up to disguise acne scars. The couple said they were leaving in a few days to look for a cottage in Ireland, having spent the previous summer there to see if they liked living on the Emerald Isle.

"Cool. Why Ireland?" I asked.

"I love to golf," the husband said.

"And I've always known I was destined to live around leper colonies," the wife said.

I told her she shouldn't be so self-conscious about her skin, at our age nobody's skin looks good and if she was really bothered by her age spots and crows' feet (which I said I thought were signs of character), I would be happy to refer her to my dermatologist.

Never got the chance to ask where in Ireland the couple intended to buy; they jumped up and ran from the table.

"She said 'leprechauns,'" my wife informed me with disgust.

And so, to make my family happy, I called an audiologist and scheduled an appointment for several weeks later.

When I arrived, the receptionist told me my appointment had been the previous day and that I had missed it. She claimed she had told me Wednesday, but I know for a fact she said Thursday. I even wrote it down.

She mumbles too. Of course, in her business, she has an incentive to.

Joe Valentine

(Published February 13, 2003) I'm just your average Joe. I read the *New York Post*. Love Kraft Macaroni & Cheese Dinner. And I haven't missed a single episode of *Joe Millionaire*, the hottest reality show of the year.

Joe is a studly construction worker who earns $19,000 a year, masquerading as a guy who just inherited $50 million. The Fox network has flown 20 bimbettes to a French chateau they have been told he owns to compete for the chance to become Mrs. Joe and share in his supposed fortune.

Each week Joe takes the bimbettes on "dates" to places like Paris, Corsica and the Riviera, and at the end of each episode, has his butler show those who have somehow displeased him the door, leaving the rest to fight like alley cats for his attention. Joe's avowed goal is to narrow the field to the one who loves him not for his money, but for who he really is deep-down—a guy who can't afford a comb—and to ask her to become his bride.

The show is a mega-hit. Women love it because Joe is handsome and virile. Men love it because Joe is living every man's fantasy—sleeping with beautiful but dumb bimbettes who are throwing themselves at him. (Hint to bimbettes: If a guy owns a chateau, he doesn't call it a chateau. *"Hey babe, let's go back to the chateau and jump in the hot tub."* He calls it a *house*).

Without having to spend a penny of his own money, Joe and his bimbettes are flying around in private jets, enjoying $1,000 dinners and shacking up in swanky hotels after which Joe gets to tell those who didn't do exactly what he wants to take a hike.

As I write this, Joe is down to two bimbettes. Inexplicably, he has kept Zora, a substitute teacher with the personality of a trout and bikini insecurity. And then there's Sarah, a gorgeous blonde who looks like Grace Kelly in *To Catch a Thief.* There's more to Sarah than meets the eye. *The Post* revealed she has appeared in fetish films.

How can Joe find out if they love him not for his money but for himself?

Take a tip from me, Joe. Spend tomorrow with them the same way I'm going to spend it with my wife. It's a ritual we've repeated six or seven times, but never on Valentine's Day.

Our celebration will officially start at 6 p.m. tonight, when, in lieu of Hershey's Kisses, I'll start popping Dulcolax laxative tablets every two hours until 2 a.m. I'll wash them down with Citroma, "the sparkling laxative," pretending it's Champagne.

I'll spend most of the night in the bathroom moaning. In the morning, my wife will find me curled up in a ball on the family room sofa.

At noon she will drive me to the hospital for my colonoscopy exam, a procedure I need annually because of a family history of unpleasantness in that particular netherworld.

She'll sit patiently in the waiting room until I wake

up from the anesthesia, by which time the doctor will have shared with her glossy photos of any polyps he found. At that point, I'll be passing approximately as much gas as the Panhandle Eastern natural gas pipeline that runs from Texas to Maine.

She will then drive me home with the car windows down as I continue to fire away...put me to bed... sequester herself across the house as far away from possible from our bedroom...and watch TV as Clyde, our dachshund, snores at her feet.

Now I know this may sound a bit extreme, Joe. But the way I see it, it's easy for a woman to fly with a guy to the south of France in a private jet, eat truffles, drink Champagne and snuggle all night under a down comforter in a luxury suite overlooking the sea. But that's not necessarily love.

Love is watching TV on the most romantic night of the year with only a dachshund to keep you company because your husband scheduled a revolting medical procedure without even considering that February 14 is Valentine's Day.

If Zora or Sarah can do that for you without complaining, congratulations — you've got yourself a keeper.

And if not?

At the very least, you'll know if you have polyps.

I'll gladly pay you tomorrow…

My wife and I belong to a Baby Boomer subset marketers call Troomers—Traumatized Boomers.

Born between 1950 and 1955, we were in grammar school during the Cuban Missile Crisis when JFK and Khrushchev were threatening to bomb the world to smithereens.

Watching Walter Cronkite's nightly reports about the crisis was traumatic enough for our tender young psyches.

Worse yet were the drills during which teachers forced us to hide under our desks and practice shielding our faces from the fallout the mushroom clouds would inevitably generate.

We weren't stupid. We watched *Mr. Wizard*. We knew the radiation would melt us like the milk chocolate in the hand that wasn't holding M&Ms.

And so, expecting to die tomorrow, and to the eternal delight of credit card companies, we Troomers have spent our adulthoods denying ourselves nothing, regardless of our ability to pay for it.

Our Florida house, which we bought this past winter, is a classic example. We saw an "open house" sign, walked in, oohed and aahed at the view, and told the agent "we'll take it."

Seemed like a good idea until the next morning when we woke up and remembered we have two kids in college, our jobs are Connecticut, and that our house up north already has a mortgage the size of Portugal's gross national product.

And on top of that, we had to furnish it from scratch.

Not having any idea how to decorate a house in the tropics, we visited the Pretentious Pointe Racquet, Golf, Yacht and Beach Club located in the heart of the Everglades somewhere between Ft. Myers and Ft. Lauderdale.

Signing ourselves into the sales office guest book as Dick and Pat Nixon (so salespeople wouldn't call), we were let loose to explore a movie-set perfect street with 10 model homes, each named after a car from the sixties or seventies—sophisticated monikers like Biscayne, Granada and Cordoba (which, when we toured it, we were disappointed to learn was lacking in rich Corinthian leather appointments).

Each house, the brochure said, had been decorated by "a different award-winning designer to whom the developer has given *carte blanche* (Florida developers like to use classy-sounding French words whenever possible) to create his or her fantasy home."

My favorite was the Edsel model, based on the decorator's favorite movies—*Godfather I* and *II*.

Brochure copy announced that this particular model was created with today's extended family in mind "because you can never lose your family."

Features included a grande leisure room with a stone fireplace like Al Pacino's and Diane Keaton's Lake Tahoe house in *Godfather II*; a study with drawn curtains like the one where Marlon Brando received callers the day his daughter, Talia Shire, got married; a dining room table set with a platter of plastic spaghetti and wine glasses filled with lucite Chianti, and a kitchen with a gold-leafed "Genco Olive Oil" valance.

My wife preferred the Bel-Air, which had been decorated to honor her favorite group, The Beatles.

This "Fab 4 BR/4BA" English tudor model included a foyer with framed gold records, a gold master suite ("where you'll enjoy countless hours of Golden Slumbers") and a Norwegian Wood-paneled library. The pool bar was in the shape of a yellow submarine.

Neither of us liked the NASCAR-themed Cutlass model with its sunken conversation "pit" living room, master bedroom suite wallpaper featuring the logos of Budweiser, Viagra, Craftsman Tools and other NASCAR sponsors, and the circular lap pool with a checkered flag finish line.

Leaving Pretentious Pointe thoroughly confused, we did what any self-respecting Troomer couple would do.

We stopped by a furniture store, hired a "design consultant" who looked to be about our age, let him take an imprint of our American Express card, gave him a key to the house, and told him to call us up north when everything was ready.

Last week we returned to a house that is, from floor to ceiling, done in shades of brown.

We hate brown.

The designer assures us our new home reflects the color palette today's sophisticated Floridian demands—colors that are "neutral" and "muted" and "relaxing."

Maybe he's right.

More likely, his favorite song was "Mrs. Brown You've Got a Lovely Daughter."

Whatever the case, the AmEx bill for our house full

of brown furniture is due in full next week.

So are both sons' tuition payments, along with estimated taxes owed to Uncle Sam and the great state of Connecticut.

Like true Troomers, we'll worry about all that then.

Hawkin' to my generation

If I ever get arthritis, I'll be damned if I'm going to ask my doctor if Celebrex is right for me.

Why? Because Celebrex commercials, which feature boomers engaging in the type of "fun" activities in which one can participate when one doesn't have arthritis pain, such as teaching impressionable children how to take credit for other people's accomplishments, drive me nuts.

Take the Celebrex spot in which a group of Boomers get together to watch their grandchildren play softball.

A beaming blonde grandma escorts her five-year-old grandson to home plate and stands behind him, wrapping her arthritis-free hands above his tiny ones on the bat, swinging with him to meet the oncoming ball so the kid won't have low self-esteem because he struck out.

The kid—not surprisingly, considering granny has better hand-eye coordination and can therefore hit a slow ball pitched by a child—smacks a home run.

Granny and her pain-free friends begin laughing hysterically, clapping and high-fiving as if they had just won the Powerball jackpot, while the kid, looking confused, runs the bases, deluding himself that he's going to be a Yankee.

Having come of age in the sixties when these folks did, I think I know why they're so exuberant.

It's not that they're feeling no joint pain because they take Celebrex.

It's the joints they fired up under the bleachers while the kids were warming up. (Note to youthful readers: I, personally, never did this, nor did your parents or anyone they know except your uncle James who is a prime example of why you shouldn't, either.)

Now, teaching kids to cheat is bad enough. But worse yet is the music that runs behind every Celebrex commercial—an elevator-music rendition of Three Dog Night's "Celebrate."

I can hear the conversation in the ad agency conference room now:

25-year-old advertising agency hotshot: *"Here's an idea. We'll buy the rights to* Celebrate—*sounds like you-know-what—and run it under each spot. Every time old farts hear the song, they'll think of Celebrex, get it?"*

31-year-old client with MBA: *"Brilliant! Tell your bosses you deserve a $50,000 bonus so you can rent a bigger house in the Hamptons next summer. And be sure to invite me out for Labor Day weekend."*

Well here's news for those of you responsible for the Celebrex campaign.

You don't take the anthem of an entire generation and use it to sell medicine to them in their dotage.

My generation loves—make that loved until you hijacked it —"Celebrate."

It was released in 1970, my first year of college.

I danced to it with my first love, a beautiful Chi-O, at my fraternity's spring formal that year.

It blasted from the eight-track tape deck of my buddy

Craig's GTO, in which we used to drive around aimlessly on warm summer nights back when the air was bursting with possibilities and so were we.

We Boomers played it at our weddings.

At our anniversaries.

For our thirtieth, fortieth, even our fiftieth birthday celebrations.

And from now on, every time we hear it, we're going to be reminded of…arthritis.

Thanks a lot.

What? You don't get my point?

OK, let me put it in simple terms even a kid like you can understand.

When you're my age, in 25 years, how would you like to see *The Simpsons* as spokespersons for, say, Depends? Lisa can be changing Homer while Marge teaches Bart, Jr. how to cheat in Monopoly. Ha-ha-ha!

The Simpsons is a cultural icon for your generation. Rock music of the sixties and seventies is, and always will be, iconic for mine.

But if you won't listen to a gray-head like me and insist on using rock songs to hawk pharmaceuticals to boomers, here's another Three Dog Night hit that'll get you an even bigger bonus than the one you got for the "Celebrate" campaign.

It's from the musical *Hair* and starts out, "How can people be so heartless? How can people be so cruel?"

The next four words—the title of the song—will be the perfect theme for Viagra, and earn you a spot in the Advertising Hall of Fame.

You say you don't know that song?

Ask your parents.

Life is too short to eat fruit

I was a fat kid. So fat I looked like Pugsley on *The Addams Family*.

How fat?

At 12, I weighed 210 pounds.

Oink, oink.

I took swimming lessons that summer with my friends Bobby, Robbie and Bobette Stuckenschneider.

Auxvasse, Mo. didn't have a municipal pool, so we had to travel to Fulton, 11 miles away. Mrs. Stuckenschneider drove us there every Saturday morning in her wide-track '59 Pontiac Ventura, a car roughly as wide as a Hummer. I occupied fully half the back seat; the Stuckenschneider kids took up the other half.

After our lessons we always stopped at the Dixie Cream donut shop.

Mrs. S. would buy her kids one hot-from-the-grease melt-in-your-mouth-I'm-salivating-like-a-rabid-raccoon-as-I-write-this glazed donut each.

I'd buy myself a dozen and eat them all on the drive home.

Then I'd have lunch.

It wasn't until I was 16 and went to military school

that I began to lose weight. Once I did, I swore I'd never pork up again. For years I refused to eat Dixie Creams or any of the hundreds of other foods I felt had contributed to my largesse.

Slowly but surely I've fallen back into the eating patterns of my youth.

This was driven home Saturday when I breakfasted in a Philadelphia hotel with my 22-year-old son.

I ordered first—a cheese omelet with home fries, side order of bacon, white toast and more cream for my coffee, please.

Ben ordered fruit.

I was incredulous. "How can the fruit of my generously-sized loins sit there and order a bowl of fruit?"

"Because I think of food as fuel," he replied calmly. "Nothing more."

I left two fries, a bite of omelet and sprig of parsley on my plate to show that I, too, am a responsible eater.

But I'm not.

Gasoline is fuel.

Food is something else.

Food is love. To wit, my mother made two loaves of bread for me during my last visit. Her 92-year-old hands kneaded the dough and shaped it into loaves. She sat at the table beaming as I ate slice after slice, slathered with damson preserves, asking anxiously if I still think she's as good a cook as she was in my Pugsley days. (I do.)

Food is escape. Like when I order the red snapper because, even though it's snowing, someone in an outdoor restaurant on St. Maarten that very second is being served a fresh-from-the-Caribbean red snapper caught by a fisherman in his brightly painted red and yellow boat.

If I shut my eyes and ignore the turtleneck wearers seated around me I can almost feel the warm breeze and hear the calypso music.

Plus, since I'm having fish, I'm entitled to key lime pie for dessert.

Food is sociability. You go out to eat with friends, to yuk it up and have fun.

The last two times we've gone out with friends we've laughed so hard fellow diners have asked us to keep it down. (Sorry about that.)

Food is comfort and joy. Mrs. Stuckenschneider's husband, Stanley, passed away last week. When mom called to provide a blow-by-blow of the funeral, she happily reported on the lavish post-burial spread served to 200 mourners by the ladies of the church—fried chicken, mashed potatoes with cream gravy, Auxvasse salad (lime Jell-O mixed with cream cheese, pecans, miniature marshmallows and melted lime sherbet) and, for dessert, Jeff Davis pie.

Mom said she had two helpings of everything. The only fruit within 10 miles in any direction was the mandarin oranges in the Jell-O.

Mom is healthy as a horse.

My father died in his fifties but it wasn't food that did him in.

My son and all those "food is fuel" people can eat their fruit but I say the hell with it.

I've been fat. I've been thin. I've been hungry most of my adult life. I've got good genetics going for me on my mother's side.

So, after years of denying myself, I've decided I'm going to eat whatever I damned well please from here on out.

If I keel over in line at Baskin-Robbins one of these hot summer nights, step over my large lifeless body and order a double Butter Pecan cone in my honor.

Life is too short to eat fruit.

Unless, of course, it's served in a Jell-O salad mixed with cream cheese, pecans, marshmallows and lime sherbet.

Fantasyland

I saw a greeting card the other day picturing two old men wearing striped shirts, plaid Bermuda shorts and black socks, sitting on a park bench, canes propped against their bony knees.

"I'm married to a 21-year-old insatiable cheerleader who can't keep her hands off me," Geezer One was telling his friend.

"So why are you crying?" asked Geezer Two.

"Because I don't remember where I live."

I bought two, crossed out "Happy Birthday you old coot" and mailed them off to my college buddies, Ted and Greg.

Both, like me, turned 50 a few years ago. And both, within the last two weeks, have e-mailed that they are getting married, for the second and fourth times respectively.

Ted's intended, Vanessa, is 28. Greg's caregiver-to-be, Cyndi, is 26.

"A very mature 26," he says.

Seems like every guy I know who's around my age is either making major changes in his life, or fantasizing about it.

My buddy Fletch came home from work one night

and announced to his wife that he wanted to quit his job as a banker and buy a coffee plantation in Honduras he found for sale on the Internet at escapeartist.com.

"Know what she did?" he asked, sounding hurt. "She laughed at me—laughed—like I was a nut case."

I understood his pain. My wife did the same thing when I tried to persuade her to move with me to Namibia in southern Africa where, for $30,000, we can build a cozy beach house with the Atlantic as our front yard and the orange sand dunes of the Namib desert as our back.

We could retire right now without having to work another 75 years to afford the lifestyle we so richly deserve.

At least my fantasy includes my wife. I couldn't live without her. How else would I be able to find my wallet and glasses every morning if she weren't there for me?

A few weeks ago I had lunch with an old fraternity brother in St. Louis where he lives with his wife and three kids, and is a deacon in his church.

"I've found the perfect woman," he announced. "She's from a small town, just like me. She's an accountant, like me. She's into French wines, skiing and first edition books. I've never met a woman I have so much in common with."

"Wow," I said tentatively, picturing his wife, who had probably held his hand as they sat in their church pew the previous Sunday, completely clueless.

"There's just one issue," he said.

"She's married too?"

"Nope. She's 29."

"So how long has this been going on?"

"Coupla months. I met her at a client lunch."

"Well, this is unexpected."

"I have to go to Chicago in a couple of weeks on business. I've reserved a suite for us at the Four Seasons but I haven't asked her yet."

"She'll go, won't she?" I asked.

"I dunno."

"Why not?"

"I don't really know her well enough to predict what she'll say."

"How often have you two, uh, gotten together?"

"Once," he replied calmly. "At that lunch I was telling you about. She had to leave before dessert."

"Let me get this straight. You've never been alone with this woman. Surely you've talked on the phone, haven't you?"

"No," he admitted, looking sheepish. "But I'm going to call her about Chicago day after tomorrow."

Flying home, I spent two hours sketching out the exterior elevation of our Namibian beach house.

I can't decide if it should have porches on both sides or just on the side facing the sea. Porches are important because, every morning, we can eat breakfast on the porch and most afternoons I plan to spend time dozing off in a wicker rocker with a dachshund on my lap.

I finally decided to build porches on both sides. Considering the ridiculously low prices for new construction in Namibia, why not?

My wife rolled her eyes when I showed her the drawings.

"There aren't any Talbot's stores in Namibia, I can't possibly move there."

I pointed out that, since she'll be living in a $30,000 house, she will be able to afford to fly back to the U.S. often and won't even have to wait for the clothes she wants to go on sale, she can pay full price.

I think that's a perfectly reasonable plan. Don't you?

Besides, I've already promised Greg and Cyndi they will be able to use the house for their honeymoon, and I don't want to disappoint them.

AARPing up the wrong tree

Friends who had already reached the half-century mark warned me I'd get it and, sure enough, they were right.

There in the mailbox the week I turned 50 was the dreaded letter from the AARP welcoming me to old-fartdom and inviting me to join for a "wide range of benefits" including a subscription to *AARP, The Magazine.*

I refused. Not because I'm loathe to admit my age (I wouldn't be writing this book if I were) but because the letter was poorly written, badly designed and printed on cheap paper. I run a direct marketing agency and make it a point never to respond to cheesy-looking solicitations.

Besides, I already get *AARP, The Magazine* at the office. My agency for some reason is on AARP's comp list. I always toss it in the circular file the moment it lands on my desk.

The other day, however, I opened it and was shocked. Not by the articles (an interview with Tony Bennett, tips for buying cheap prescription drugs in Mexico, a story about geriatric Harley-riders) but the ads.

Take the one from The Hartford Insurance offering a free booklet, "At the Crossroads: A Guide to Alzheimer's Disease, Dementia and Driving." The copy says that "deciding when to limit or stop driving can be a difficult issue for individuals diagnosed with dementia and their caregivers."

Not to mention a difficult issue for the people they run down in their Mercury Grand Marquis sedans.

An ad for Plavis, a drug that prevents blood clots, announces, "You don't want another heart attack or another stroke to sneak up on you."

No I don't. Nor do I want to see two "anothers" in the same sentence.

The ad pictures a silver-haired dude with a backpack standing at the edge of the Grand Canyon. If I'm going to have "another heart attack or another stroke," that's where I want to have it, so I can hurl myself over the side before the pain becomes unbearable.

Sun City Communities by Del Web promises, "your best is yet to come."

I somehow doubt that. My best was the summer of my twentieth year spent in Sweden camping under the northern lights with a Dutch girl who wore bib overalls with nothing underneath. If Sun City can make that happen again, I'll buy one of their condos in a heartbeat. Heck, I'll even buy an attached villa.

The older woman in a muumuu standing happily beside the Sleep Number Bed ("trusted by chiropractors, loved by sore, achy backs") looks familiar.

Wait a moment. That's no ordinary older woman. It's the *Bionic Woman*, Lindsay Wagner, "actress, mom, gardener."

Gardener?

I'm afraid to turn the page for fear I might find Farrah Fawcett endorsing Polident.

Here is an ad inviting me to attend "Life@50," the

AARP's gala national convention in Chicago, where I can be entertained by the likes of Debbie Reynolds, Dr. Phil and Dr. Ruth.

Personally, I'd rather have a prostatectomy.

Luckily, I see I'll never have to, thanks to an alternative prostate treatment called Theraseed whose slogan is, "Remember the name, forget the cancer."

What 28-year-old MBA moron marketing manager approved that line?

Senekot *("Our family of Senekot laxatives are* – sic – *made exclusively for your family")* invites me to "choose a laxative for the people you love that'll treat them as gently as you do."

How does Senekot know I treat the people I love gently? Maybe I'm into roughage.

And why can't the people I love choose their own damn laxatives? Do I have to do everything for them? Jeez.

Speaking of which, I'm reminded of a story the advertising manager of Ex-Lax, the chocolate-flavored laxative, told me years ago. (When you're my age, everything reminds you of a story from 20 years ago because you can't remember what happened yesterday.)

Ex-Lax received a complaint letter from a boss who was outraged that a disgruntled employee on her last day had brought to the office a beautiful chocolate cake. She didn't tell anyone it was frosted with melted Ex-Lax. Everyone had a piece. He had two.

The office was shut down for three days.

End-user experiences

Philips, the Netherlands-based electronics manufacturer, has finally admitted something the rest of the world has known for years.

Its products are so complicated nobody can figure out how to operate them.

So, in an inspired marketing move, the company has announced plans to build products people can actually use.

"Our route to innovation isn't about extra complexity—it's about simplicity which we believe will be the new cool," says the company's CEO.

A press release elaborates that Philips' goal is to "give customers a distinctive image of a sharper, more focused enterprise, which...is held together by a common drive to deliver intuitive end-user experiences."

These people can't even write understandable press releases so I'm not holding out a lot of hope here.

Besides, even if they succeed, I won't be able to use their products because I'm a product of another era—the Jurassic era before everything was controlled by microchips when (I swear this is true, kids) people *actually had to get up off the sofa to change channels*, which was accomplished by turning a plastic knob.

Whereas babies today come out of the womb holding

giant universal remotes they already know how to use (one reason more women are opting for C-sections), I can't figure out anything electronic.

Take our VCR. I paid extra for a feature called VCR Plus which is supposed to work like this: You see a program listed in *TV Guide* that you want to tape…a code is printed next to the program name…you enter that code into the VCR and…abracadabra, it records the show.

None of the ads revealed that, prior to taping anything, you have to program the VCR with codes representing the cable company's various channels. Those codes, naturally, don't correlate to the numbers that appear on the cable box.

Because I couldn't, my brother kindly spent an entire day programming the codes.

The next day, the power went out, the VCR "forgot" them all, and has been flashing "12:00" ever since.

That was 10 years ago.

At least I was able to use the VCR to view rented movies. But now most movies come on DVD. So I bought a DVD player. My teenager hooked it up to the VCR which is hooked up to the cable box which is hooked up to the TV, don't ask me how.

Last weekend when I wanted to watch a movie, I had to call him at college to walk me through the process, which involved programming the TV to "accept" the signal from the DVD player. After 15 minutes, I said forget it.

Then there's my 116-function cell phone. My old one which, when I turned it in to Cingular, was supposedly going to be donated to a shelter for battered women (as if they need more problems) displayed a message that said I had 178 unlistened-to calls in my in-box. I never had figured out how to retrieve them. My new phone is up to 43. Maybe one is from Lotto telling me I have to claim my jackpot or lose it. I'll never know.

Our microwave oven is as easy to program as, say, a guided missile. After five years I still I can't figure out how the timer works.

Luckily I've learned that hitting the "popcorn" button produces a perfect cup of instant coffee and "baked potato" is great for nuking Kraft Easy Mac.

Most frustrating of all is the high-tech luxury sedan I recently bought to replace my low-tech convertible. The first six months I owned it, the car ran out of gas four times, even though the gauge said there was plenty of fuel.

I returned it to the dealer's shop. The service people laughed at me when I came to pick it up. They said I must be reading the fuel gauge incorrectly because they had hooked up the car's computer to their master computer and it didn't indicate anything wrong. I assured them I'm perfectly capable of reading a damned fuel gauge.

After three more incidents, they finally determined a computer chip was defective.

Even the car's clock is impossibly complex. Sunday before last I spent 30 minutes trying to figure out how to re-set it to standard time. I finally gave up. I'll just deduct an hour from the time it displays until April. (Or should I add an hour? I'm never sure about these things.)

My next car is going to be a simple '57 Chevy. I have been searching for one on eBay but my computer keeps freezing, and asking if I want it to send an error message to Microsoft.

I do indeed. And the message I want it to send is not

only for Microsoft, it's for Sanyo, Sharp, Philips, Daimler-Chrysler and all those other companies whose overcomplicated products are the primary reason I have to take blood pressure medication.

Bite me.

Alice doesn't eat here any more

I had business recently in Ft. Lauderdale. Arriving the night before, hungry and craving salt air, I decided to have dinner at an outdoor restaurant on the waterfront near my hotel.

A few moments after I was seated, a well-dressed Gen X couple and their daughter, who looked to be about four, were shown to Table 7 in front of mine.

The wife, I couldn't help but notice, was wearing a diamond ring the size of my eyeball.

The little girl took a coloring book and crayons out of her knapsack, and began to color.

The waitress, who reminded me of what Tipper Gore might have looked like if she had married a shiftless husband who drank half her tips, explained to the family that night's specials, and asked what they would like to drink.

"What brands of bottled water do you have?" the wife asked.

"We only have Dasani," the waitress replied.

"If that's all you have, I guess it will have to do," the wife said with a sigh. "Bring it with a slice of lime, in a glass with no ice."

While the drinks were being fetched, the wife studied the menu with the intensity of someone reading a newspaper account about an axe murder in her own neighborhood.

When the waitress returned, she asked if they were ready to order.

The wife gestured for her husband to go ahead. He ordered a Caesar salad and mahi-mahi.

"Are you ready, ma'am?" the waitress asked.

"Talk to me about the chicken fingers on the children's menu. How are they prepared?"

"They're deep-fried."

"Well that's no good, we don't eat fried foods do we Alice?" the wife half-asked, half-told the child and everyone else within earshot, in a tone that would have been appropriate had she learned the restaurant was serving fried rat and passing it off as chicken fingers. "Tell the chef to broil them."

"Ma'am, they're frozen and breaded. If he removed the breading, there wouldn't be anything left to broil."

"Well then," she snapped, "What would you suggest I feed my daughter?"

"How about a cheeseburger?"

"Alice doesn't eat red meat, do you Alice?"

Alice didn't look up from her coloring book.

"Forget it. Bring two plates and she'll share my entree. Talk to me about the sea bass. Is it fresh?"

"Yes ma'am."

"How do you know, did you catch it yourself?"

"No ma'am, but all our fish is fresh."

"Does it have skin?"

"Yes, it does."

"Tell the chef to remove it before he grills it, and to make sure it's cooked all the way through."

"Okay, I'll speak with him personally when I take the

order to the kitchen."

"Does he put butter on it?"

"Not if you don't want it."

"No butter, no oil. Just a lemon wedge. We don't eat butter, do we Alice?"

Alice continued coloring.

"Alright ma'am, will there be anything else?"

"A baked potato. Not too well done, I don't want the skin crispy."

"Sour cream?"

"No, just non-fat yogurt on the side with some chives."

"I'm sorry, we don't have yogurt."

"You don't have yogurt?"

"No ma'am, I've never had anyone ask for it."

"Well they have it in all the good restaurants where I come from!"

"And where would that be?"

"Saddle Ridge, New Jersey."

"Well then," the waitress replied sweetly, "I suggest you go back there to eat, because I've worked in restaurants from Pensacola to Key West and I don't think there's one in the state of Florida that can make you happy."

The waitress leaned down, swooped up their drinks, put them on her tray, did an about-face and walked back into the kitchen.

"Mommy, I'm hungry," Alice wailed.

"Nice job Barbara, "the husband said, wearily. "That's the second time this month. Has it ever occurred to you that the world doesn't revolve around what you put in your mouth?"

"I'm going back to the hotel and order from room

service," the wife announced. "C'mon Alice."

Alice placed her coloring book back in the knapsack, and handed it to her mother who stood up, took the child's hand and stormed out. The husband followed.

Oh…and if you're worried the waitress didn't earn a tip from Table 7 that night? Don't be.

The one I left her more than made up for it.

The crude truth

SUVs whose drivers pull up to my right when I'm trying to turn left, blocking my view of oncoming traffic, make me angry.

Want to know what really sends me to the moon?

Monster SUVs—Lexus 470s, Cadillac Escalades, Hummers, Infiniti QX56s, Chevy Suburbans and Lincoln Aviators—with yellow "Support Our Troops" ribbons proudly displayed on the back.

They're everywhere.

The other day I was driving down the highway when a Lexus 470 with a "Support Our Troops" ribbon blew past me at 80 mph.

That vehicle, according to Lexus' web site, comes with a standard 32-valve V-8 engine that gets a whopping 13 miles per gallon in the city, 17 mpg on the open highway.

Here's my personal message for the driver of that behemoth, and for the drivers of other monster SUVs who believe that affixing a "Support" ribbon shows they care.

If you really supported our troops you'd pull your vehicle over to the side of the road and torch it.

Think about it. (I know, I know. You don't want to

think about it because you love your mega-SUV—but do it anyway.)

It's a fact that the troops you so proudly support are in the Middle East to fight terrorism.

It's also a fact—one nobody likes to talk about but everyone with half a brain knows—that America has fought two wars in that particular part of the world in the last 15 years in large part to assure a nonstop supply of oil to feed our nation's addiction to fossil fuels.

"But," you say. "I'm special. I *need* a vehicle that size."

Well here's a news flash.

You are not special.

I don't care how much sports equipment you have to haul around.

I don't care how much space you want to put between you and your noisy kids.

I don't care how steep your driveway is.

I don't give a rat's you-know-what if you have to drive up to your ski condo in Vermont every winter weekend.

If you need a four-wheel drive vehicle, you can get a Subaru, Ford Escape (the new Hybrid model gets up to 33 mpg on the highway), a Jeep, a Blazer or something that doesn't drink fuel like a 747.

If there were a limitless supply of oil and we weren't at war to secure it, you could drive your behemoth with a clear conscience.

But there isn't. And we are.

And what have you done about it?

You've festooned your gas-guzzler with a cute little ribbon. And the hypocrisy of what you've done doesn't occur to you as you happily drive around in a vehicle roughly half the size of Montana.

During WWII, Americans gave up things that were in short supply to support the war effort. Sixty years later we run out and buy ribbons to tie around our trees, wear on our lapels or to display on our vehicles.

Kumbayah.

You say I'm making you uncomfortable? How can Tommy Wommie be so meanie-wienie when all you are trying to do by affixing the ribbon is to show how much you care?

Good. It's about time you faced up to the fact that we're at war and driving a Suburban or Hummer or whatever monster truck you're driving is tantamount to driving around in a Mercedes during WWII.

Once you start making sacrifices—turning down the heat, switching to fuel-efficient vehicles—you will be truly be supporting our troops.

Until that day comes, by all means drive your Lexus 470, Cadillac Escalade (12-16 mpg), Hummer (9 mpg), Infiniti QX56 (12-15 mpg) Lincoln Aviator (13-18 mpg) or Suburban (14-18 mpg). It's your right. This is America.

But do the rest of us a favor.

Take the Support Our Troops ribbon off of it.

If you really want to support our troops get down on your knees tonight and pray to God to keep them safe and bring them home as soon as possible.

While you're at it, ask Him to give you some common sense.

Ol' Blue Eyes is back

My wife has never, ever, misplaced *anything*.

She knows where everything she owns is at this very moment including the rhinestone "Miss Hannibal" tiara she won the night she was voted the most comely and talented lass in Hannibal, Mo. (She's still bitter about losing the Miss Missouri crown to a cross-eyed girl who tap-danced to "Raindrops Keep Falling On My Head." But I digress.)

Naturally, she married her polar opposite. Keeping track of possessions isn't one of my priorities. Even if it were, it would be impossible since, every night while we're asleep, someone breaks into the house and maliciously hides my wallet, glasses, cell phone and/or keys, moving them from where I carefully left them on the coffee table, kitchen counter or breakfast room hutch.

I don't get concerned when I can't find them—everything the intruder hides eventually reappears.

My wife, on the other hand, worries herself sick that they will never be found, and turns the house upside-down until she locates whatever is missing.

Take our recent weekend trip to Florida. We were scheduled to fly out of Newark.

I had lots on my mind the morning we left. I had to

lock the doors, turn out the lights and back the car out of the garage. I sat in it listening to news radio as my wife double-checked what I'd already done. The traffic reporter said the GW bridge was a mess so I was preoccupied thinking about the best route to Newark from the Tappan Zee.

"Where are your glasses?" my wife asked as we were breezing down the Merritt Parkway. "You almost hit a guard rail there." (That's something else she worries about unnecessarily—my driving. I haven't received a ticket all year.)

"I broke them last week," I replied truthfully. (Despite what it says on my license, it's not like I need to wear them all the time. As long as I can see the car ahead of me I'm fine.)

She insisted I pull over and let her drive.

Once we arrived, she became irrational when, in the parking lot, I couldn't find my wallet. I was sure I had left it under the car seat the night before. I often leave it there if I haven't placed it on the powder room sink, on the desk in the den, or on our bedroom dresser.

"You've gotta have photo ID. They're not going to let you board."

"Just watch," I said confidently, heading toward the terminal. "I don't look like a terrorist. Terrorists don't have blue eyes. Besides, I was Missouri president of the Children of the American Revolution in 1965. They can call my mother for confirmation."

I showed the airline agent the book I was carrying. "All I have is this book from the Wilton Library. The library is owned by the town of Wilton, Conn., which, of course, has its own government which issues IDs including library cards. You can't check a book out of the library unless you have a card, so I clearly have a card but it was in my wallet which, unfortunately, some lowlife stole."

The agent wouldn't buy it. "Do you have an insurance card?"

"Not any more. I had one but it was in my wallet."

"I do!" my wife piped up, her voice shaking with relief. "It's my card but has his name on it."

The agent reluctantly issued my boarding pass. "I can't guarantee you'll get through security."

But we did.

I flashed my blue eyes at the female TSA agent and held out my wife's driver's license, which I placed on top of the insurance card with my name. She waved us through.

My wife stewed all the way to Florida. When we landed, Avis claimed they needed my driver's license to give me the car I had reserved. "I've rented from you 50 times," I protested, but they wouldn't budge.

My wife had to rent the car in her name then refused to let me drive it, even though I knew exactly where we were going and she didn't.

All weekend she kept reminding me I was ruining her trip, she had knots in her stomach and that I'd probably be denied boarding for the return flight.

The day we were to fly home, she lectured me all the way to the airport. She said she wasn't my mother (it would be disturbing not to mention illegal if she were; we have two children), that I was a grown man, it wasn't her responsibility to keep track of my things and that she was sick and tired after all these years of my irresponsibility. By God, she was boarding that plane and going home whether they let me board or not, she didn't care.

But my charms and the insurance card trick worked at the Florida airport, too.

And now, Ol' Blue Eyes is back home in Connecticut where my wife, as I knew she would, found my wallet. The intruder had hidden it in the pocket of a pair of slacks in the dirty clothes hamper.

Even I am getting tired of his antics and really should call the police to report him. Unfortunately, he hid my cell phone last week. But I'm not worried.

It'll show up soon.

You've got mail.
(Not to mention an amazing Venus.)

I arrived at the office this morning and, as usual, checked my e-mail first thing.

Among the messages that had arrived overnight were notes from two clients; news from my mother reporting the progress of workers repaving her driveway; a joke forwarded by my buddy Ed, and an invitation to try a "revolutionary herbal pill guaranteed to grow your (rhymes with Venus) down to your knees."

I opened that one. After all, what man wouldn't like to be the undisputed King of the Locker Room?

Granted, my enhanced Venus might be distracting to other shoppers when I go to the local supermarket in summer, because I generally wear shorts during hot weather. What's more, I'd have to take all my slacks to the tailor for alterations.

But I'm not going to rule out the possibility, at least not yet.

All in all, it was a typical day's e-mail.

Every day I receive something like 50 e-mails, of which at least 30 are spam from people I don't know, containing bizarre offers I don't want to know about. How they get my e-mail address I haven't a clue. Here's a smattering from today's mailbox.

"Dr. Evil" invites me to order "a one-of-a-kind sampling of the greatest lovemaking tunes, featuring 18 smashing love grooves brought to you by the man himself: Austin Powers."

Shagadelic, baby.

"Did you leave your boxers under my bed last night?" asks someone named Monique.

Hmm, let's see. I had dinner at Taco Bell because my wife was out, then dropped off my dry cleaning. I can't even remember meeting you, Monique, but maybe I did. Perhaps I should order those Ginkgo capsules featured in the e-mail just below yours that will "help improve your memory by 85 percent."

And for the record, I don't own boxers. I own dachshunds.

"A Special Message from United Airlines" announces that United has filed for Chapter 11 but that they want me to know "we will CONTINUE TO FLY A SAFE AND RELIABLE AIRLINE."

That's swell, guys. Now if you could just find my luggage you lost six years ago.

"Tom Dryden, you can increase your bustline by 4-8 inches in less than two weeks!" proclaims a message from Tittianna@hotmail.com.

No thanks Tittianna. I'm already embarrassed to take off my shirt at the beach. That would send me over the edge.

Nine different spammers are inviting me to take advantage of the "lowest mortgage rates in years."

And here's great news from one of them: "Your (sic) pre-approved."

"The greatest love ever!!!!" reads the headline on a

message from Susan@supernet, who informs me that "after 42 years of struggling with the meaning of life, I met a man named Jesus and He changed my life."

I'm happy for you, Susan—I really am—but I was hoping you were one of Monique's girlfriends.

And here's something to think about. When Jesus instructed His disciples to go out and spread the word, He wasn't talking about spam.

Someone named Demetrius Samara promises that, for a mere $9.99 a month, he will teach me how to "SCORE WITH HOT BABES IN SECONDS."

Where were you when I was 22?

Kafasde3547 wants to pay me "up to $40 an hour for dining at my favorite restaurants."

Now that's intriguing. But I'd probably pack on unwanted pounds.

Luckily, just below that message is one for a diet on which I can "lose up to 4.5 percent of your total body weight" in two days. Reading on, I see I'll have to "drink four quarts of water daily plus one additional glass for every 25 pounds of excess weight."

No way I can drink that much water. Now that I'm over 50, my bladder isn't as strong as it used to be.

Plus, if I order those Venus pills, I'm going to be nervous about using public men's rooms.

If you were packing a Venus like the one I'm gonna have, wouldn't you be?

A night at the Molokai

We never made it to the game.

There we were, in a seedy beach bar beneath a low-rent high-rise cinder block hotel, listening to the waitress describe the old man in a toupee the bouncer had tossed during happy hour for exposing himself to a lady tourist.

And the night was still young.

My cousin Bill and I were best buds as kids, but rarely get to see each other these days, so we recently made arrangements to meet in Ft. Myers, Fla., where his twin sons' college hockey team was scheduled to play at a nearby arena. Bill brought along his 25-year-old daughter, an auburn-haired Priscilla Presley lookalike named Rachel.

As we were driving past the Molokai Inn, en route to the game, one of his sons called Bill's cell phone. Both boys had missed the team bus and were still in Georgia.

They weren't going to be playing, so we decided to bag the game.

Which is why, moments later, we were sitting at the Molokai bar while the waitress rambled on about the drunken flasher, her deadbeat ex-husbands and the good-as-new 1996 model mobile home she had just rented.

A few feet away, a fifty-ish blonde wearing black

shorts and a ribbed tank top over a stomach that looked eight months pregnant danced by herself to "I Will Survive."

"I think she has the hots for you two," Rachel joked.

We ordered Pain-In-The-Asses—half rum-runners, half pina coladas—topped with 151-proof rum served in tall plastic glasses.

After several rounds we decided to cross the street to the Beached Whale for dinner. Rachel's drink was nearly full, so she brought it along.

On the way we stopped at a 7-Eleven. Rachel left her drink outside the entrance atop a newspaper vending machine.

A bum who looked like he could have belonged to Z.Z. Topp appeared out of the shadows, grabbed Rachel's Pain-In-The-Ass and gulped it down. Bill rushed out. "Hey, that's my daughter's drink."

"Yer dog's drink? Dogs don't need no drinks. I need drinks."

The manager chased him away. "I've had to call the po-lice twice tonight. He keeps coming around trying to steal beer."

We ate greasy burgers at the Whale and headed back toward the Molokai, stopping at a bar where a country-western band was playing to a rowdy crowd.

"Tonight's the night ya'll sit yer clocks back an hour, so yew kin party longer," the lead singer announced as he segued into "Mamas Don't Let Your Babies Grow Up To Be Cowboys."

We went next door to a karaoke bar. Bill got up and sang "Brown Eyed Girl." I sang "Satisfaction." (Or maybe "Jumping Jack Flash"—I'm almost sure it was a Stones song.)

When we got back to the Molokai, a band was blasting Roy Orbison. The bar was packed with bikers. Over-served, over-sunned tourists were dirty dancing. The tank top blonde was still dancing by herself. A disturbingly thin woman in a long black dress was working the crowd, piercing navels for $39.

We took a pass when she offered to do ours.

When we stumbled back to our car at 2:30 a.m., it was gone.

A security guard approached. "Brown Avis Buick? I watched Brillo's Towing tow it away an hour ago. You was in the guest lot, you need a permit sticker after midnight."

We called Brillo's and were assured the car would reappear in 20 minutes provided we could cough up $100 cash, which we could.

"See that balcony?" the guard asked, pointing to the sixth floor of the Molokai. "Last year a couple from Cape Coral come here for their 30th anniversary. Beats me why anyone would stay at this dump, it's fulla sand fleas. Anyways, they get drunked up, start fightin' and he pushes her backwards over the rail. Holds her by her legs while she's cussin' and screamin' bloody murder then drops her head-first, yells 'good riddance' as she hits the parkin' lot, and goes back in the room 'till the po-lice come."

"Did she die?" Rachel asked.

"Yup. Head exploded like a watermelon. Saw it myself."

The tow truck arrived with the car. The driver, a short man with a shaved head, tattoos and hoop earrings hopped out. We paid him the ransom and he set the Buick free.

"You have a good evening," he said to the gray-haired men leaving the sleaze-bag hotel with the auburn-haired beauty.

"We already did," we laughed, feeling 21 and knowing darn well we wouldn't in the morning.

Prisoners of love

It is said that men are from Mars and women are from Venus.

Bull.

We're not even from the same solar system.

This was driven home the other night as I watched *20/20*. Barbara Walters was interviewing the beautiful blonde who married Eric Menendez.

Eric, as you may recall, is the younger of the two Menendez brothers, who mounted one of the most creative defenses in criminal history.

At ages 18 and 20, they suddenly realized their wealthy parents were child rapists and threatened to go public with this information.

The parents, naturally, announced plans to kill their sons to keep them quiet.

Fearing for their lives, the brothers snuck up with a shotgun as the parents were eating strawberries and cream in the family room of their Beverly Hills mansion, and fired repeatedly.

They then went on a shopping spree to forget their grief, buying Rolex watches, Porsches and other goodies with their parents' millions.

Their first trial ended with a hung jury.

The second time around, they got life with no possibility of parole.

Mrs. Eric—Tammi—told Barbara her inspiring story. She was an ordinary Minnesota housewife, married to a man who wasn't around for her emotionally when she needed him. Fascinated by the Menendez Brothers' trial on Court TV, Tammi began corresponding with Eric in prison.

After the death of her husband (she never said what he died of, but I would imagine he died of embarrassment, knowing his wife was writing Eric), she started dating a wealthy doctor, but couldn't stop thinking about Eric, with whom she was falling head over heels in love.

So, she told the doctor to take a hike and, using the proceeds from her dead husband's insurance, moved to Sacramento, where she bought a house with a swimming pool and a Mercedes SUV, to be near her Prince Charming.

Three years ago she married Eric in the prison visiting room. In lieu of a wedding cake, they shared a vending machine Twinkie.

Tammi now spends her days visiting Eric, and, when they're apart, reading his love letters and chatting with him on the phone about their favorite TV shows which she watches in her swell house and he watches in the Big House. She says she's deliriously happy, and that he's her soul mate (not to mention her inmate). Why, he even reads stories to her six-year-old daughter on visiting days!

I ask you, would a man ever do that? If it had been the Menendez sisters—Erica and Lila—do you think there's a man on earth who would have married one of them?

No way.

Men know that a woman incarcerated for life can't make dinner or do laundry, nor can she perform her most important wifely duty—getting out of the car at gas stations and asking attendants for directions when her husband is hopelessly lost.

A man wouldn't put up with an imprisoned woman for one minute, much less marry one. But women marry male inmates all the time.

Ladies, I may be betraying my Martian species, but here's a tip. You want a man who will always be there for you? A man who will do whatever you want? Try this.

You: "Darling, wanna go to the movies tonight?"

Your husband: "No thanks, I'm tired from getting up at five and working all day. Can't we stay home?"

You: "Fine. Eric Menendez is taken, but I'm going to start writing his brother, Lyle. You'll die of humiliation. With your insurance money, I'm going to take the kids and move to California. I'll buy a Mercedes SUV so I can drive back and forth to prison to visit him. Then I'm going on *20/20* and tell Barbara Walters you weren't there for me when I needed you. What's more, I'm going to give an interview to the local paper; it'll appear on the front page along with a picture of Lyle and me in color, eating a Ding-Dong."

Trust me when I say he'll be your prisoner for life.

Hometown banking with the personal touch

RING RING.
Hello.
Mr. Thomas Dryden please.
Speaking.
Good evening Mr. Dryden, my name is Demetrius. I'm calling from Second Dominion of Lower New England and Mojave National Bank, your hometown bank with the personal touch. According to our records, you conducted a transaction yesterday at your local branch located in Wilton, C-T.
Yes, is there some problem?
Not at all. Mr. Dryden as your hometown bank, Second Dominion is committed to providing the personal, attentive service you deserve, so I am calling to take a brief survey about your experience. What type of transaction did you conduct?
I deposited a check for $25.
Did you deposit it with a teller, into a lobby drop box or ATM, or at the drive-through window?
Drive-through.
On a scale of one to ten, with ten representing your complete satisfaction and one representing your extreme

dissatisfaction, how would you rate the experience?

A ten.

That's terrific. Now, a few more questions if you don't mind.

Look, I have to go, My wife is gagging in the dining room, I think she's choking on a chicken bone.

Would there be a convenient time to call back?

She's waving her arms and turning blue. How many more questions?

Just a few, I promise.

Her hands are around her throat, her eyes are bulging out of their sockets. It reminds me of when Liz Taylor almost choked to death at that dinner when she was married to John Warner, remember that?

It'll take just a moment.

You're in luck. She just fell face down in her mashed potatoes and doesn't seem to be breathing, so fire away.

On a scale of one to ten, with ten representing excellent and one representing completely unsatisfactory, how would you rate the teller who served you on the following criteria: Courtesy?

Three. She growled like a wolf and bared her teeth.

Professionalism?

Well, she whipped off her blouse and smashed her chest against the window. I wouldn't call that professional behavior for a banker, so I'd have to give her a two in that department. Would have been a six if she weren't 70 years old, and a ten if she were built like Anna Nicole Smith, but she wasn't.

Personal appearance and hygiene?

A one. Her breath was so bad I could smell it through the loudspeaker. Had to have my car fumigated.

Thank you Mr. Dryden. As you are undoubtedly

aware, effective June 30, Second Dominion of Lower New England and Mojave is merging with Third Nebraska Hawaiian Bank of the Confederacy to serve you even better. During this time, you may experience some minor inconvenience as we convert our current systems over to those of Third Nebraska.

What kind of inconvenience?

I'm not sure, Mr. Dryden.

So why are you telling me this?

It's in my script, Mr. Dryden.

Is my money going to be accessible or not?

Would you like me to connect you to my supervisor?

No, but this is the seventh time in ten years your bank has merged and every time I've had to get a new account number, have new checks printed up, and memorize a new PIN for the ATM. It's a pain.

I understand, Mr. Dryden. Just one last question

Sure, but go fast, I'm looking out the window. A tornado just hit the house next door and is moving this way.

What does C-T stand for?

Connecticut.

Oh, I thought it might be Kentucky.

Kentucky starts with "K."

I see. Well, on behalf of all of us, including the staff of your branch in Wilton, C-T, thank you for banking with Second Dominion of Lower New England and Mojave, your hometown bank with the personal touch. Have a nice evening.

No place to go but up

To: Our Valued Employees
From: K.B. Ebberlay, CEO

It is my sad duty to inform you that this morning, Worldadelphiaron filed for reorganization under Chapter 11 of the U.S. Bankruptcy Code.

As you may be aware, several weeks ago a temporary receptionist on assignment in our Paducah office discovered an accounting impropriety, which was immediately brought to the attention of myself and our board of directors.

As a result, it became necessary to restate our revenues for the years 1998-2005.

I was as shocked and disappointed as any of you to learn that, rather than earning $675 billion during this period as had been reported to shareholders, we had actually lost more than twice that amount.

This news sent the value of our stock, in which many of you—and, I might add, my wife Gloria and I—had invested for the "golden" years, into a sharp decline.

I know you may feel betrayed and want to kick somebody—preferably somebody in the Accounting Department whose initials are T.R.M. I know that many of you will be humiliated when well-meaning neighbors leave clothing and casseroles on your doorsteps, assuming that because you work for us, you can no longer afford your own. These feelings are only natural. Frankly, I have them, too.

But I want to assure you of this: We are going to emerge from these difficult times a stronger company, an enterprise better prepared for the future.

Here are a few of the steps we are taking, effective immediately, to ensure that our company will not only survive, but continue to thrive.

1. Our CFO has been terminated, and a strong warning letter has been added to the personnel file of our Controller.

2. With the repossession of many of our plants, warehouses, office facilities, and my administrative assistant's breast implants, it has become necessary to rethink our company's role as a leader in the global marketplace. Accordingly, I have appointed a committee to draft a new mission statement. You will be among the first to know our new mission once it is determined.

3. We are cooperating fully with the SEC, FBI, GQ, USAF and CBGB. If you see representatives of these organizations in the hallways, please give them a warm Worldadelphiaron "hi" on my behalf. Unfortunately, I will not be on hand to welcome them myself. I will be in our Bermuda office meeting with securities analysts and creditors, to reassure them about the direction of our company.

4. We are reallocating human resources. Approximately 71,507 of our valued Associates will be receiving invitations to group meetings to be held tomorrow at 11 a.m. Do not be concerned about the cardboard boxes

mailroom employees will be leaving outside your offices tonight. They are for your convenience in tossing unused files and other documents. We're going to be a leaner, meaner organization...with no baggage from our past to bog us down!

5. We will be actively negotiating with other companies to assume our annual $200 million payment for the title rights to the Worldadelphiaron Arena.

On a personal note, my wife, Gloria, has opened a thrift shop on Rodeo Drive. Present your employee I.D. and you will receive 10 percent off any one item. (Limit: One discount per employee per day. Offer does not apply to jewelry from the Marie Antoinette collection, Bedermeier furniture or Monet paintings.)

If you are confident about our future—and you have every reason to be—I hope you will help us spread the message to our customers and will help us attract new ones.

I can only tell you I wasn't there for past indiscretions—as you may have read in the latest issue of *Town and Country,* Gloria and I spend our springs and summers in Montana, autumns in Mustique and winters in Aspen—but I will commit to being there for future ones. And I hope you'll be by my side.

God bless America. And God bless Worldadelphiaron!

A song of myselves

I've never met another Tom Dryden.
Never wanted to.
I like to think I'm a one-of-a-kind.
But with six billion people on earth, the odds are nil that I'm the only one.
So one rainy Saturday I entered my name at google.com, the Internet search engine, to locate other Tom Drydens, past and present.
The earliest Tom Dryden I found was born in 1563 in Northampton, England.
One of his descendants, Tommy Dryden, married a lass named Priscilla Dick, sister of the unfortunately-named Minnie Dick.
I bet Minnie hated her parents
In 1843, a ship, the Thomas Dryden, sank in Scotland's Pentland Firth, inspiring a really bad poem:

She was tossed about the merciless sea
And received some terrible shocks.
Until at last she ran against
A jagged reef of rocks.

Too bad Tom Dryden of the Texas Offshore Performance Powerboat Squadron dedicated to "promoting boating safety, racing and fellowship," wasn't at the helm.

A website created by a Brit named Potter contains a touching tribute to his uncle, Pvt. Tom Dryden, a member of the 2/4th Battalion of the Duke of Wellington's Regiment, who was killed in France in WWI, three days before the Armistice.

Rest in peace, Tom. And thanks.

From the other side of the world, the Military Activity Office of Subic Bay, Philippines reports, "the mayor has instituted restrictive policies on bars. No more go-go girls or elevated stages, no alcohol from 0200-0900. Some owners subsequently moved to Subic City." But one stayed put: "Tom Dryden's Bar, Karaoke and Poker Room."

In Edinburgh, Scotland, Tom Dryden is an expert on heating and cooling systems at Dryden Aqua, "the largest web store in the world for water treatment industries."

Up in Calgary, Canada, Tom Dryden runs a company called Ammonite.com," manufacturer of gemstones, prepared from a rare mineral deposited on the surface of fossiled Ammonites, originating 400 million years ago."

A smart Tom Dryden. Probably rich, too.

A fictional Tom Dryden "found mutilated and dying in the village churchyard" is the victim of a serial killer in a novel entitled "Whoever Has a Heart."

Actor Tom Dryden landed a bit role on *Night Caller* in 1988 and, in 1999, played a cop on *Nash Bridges*.

Hope he has a day job to pay the bills between gigs.

A Tom Dryden to whom I can't possibly be related won "First in Decorative Birds of Prey" in the 2002

Ontario Wildlife Woodcarving competition

And the Glassaholics Club in Lakeland, Florida had a thrilling program in store for members in February: "Tom Dryden will be bringing samples from his collection of Vaseline glass and explaining all about this colorful glass."

I don't even want to know.

In Haltwhistle, England, one Tom Dryden is "superintendent of the workhouse, built in 1839 to hold 60 inmates."

Down the road in Gateshead, another is chair of Governors at St. Augustine Primary School where, according to inspectors, "pupils are extremely polite, friendly and have a clear sense of right and wrong."

Way to go, Tom.

Tom Dryden, a collector of Japanese woodprints, asks on an antiques message board, "I have what may be a real Hangaro/Mizuimon. Can anyone recommend a reliable expert?"

If he's the actor Tom, I hope for his sake it's real—he probably needs the cash.

A Montgomery County, Mo. historical website relates this story from the 1880s. "Thomas Dryden was a leading member of the Methodist church, but one day needed some whisky, went to Danville and procured a jugful of that fiery liquid. On his way home he met his pastor, who was bitterly opposed to intoxicating liquors. Dryden wondered what he should do—he, a church steward, with a jug of whisky! But a happy thought struck him. He remembered the pastor had once entertained the Governor and had sent to the saloon for a bottle when the Governor had called for a stimulant. When they met, the pastor asked, 'Well, Brother Dryden, what is that you have in your jug?' Dryden answered, 'It's some whisky I have just purchased for the Governor, who is at my house.'"

Now that's a Tom Dryden I can definitely relate to. I'm named after that one.

A little less conversation

After much soul-searching and prayer, I have come to the conclusion that the death penalty is so cruel and unusual that it should be administered only to those for whom there is no hope that they will ever be able to make positive contributions to society.

I'm speaking, of course, of people who go around in public wearing strap-on cell phones with microphones suspended in front of their faces, making them look like deranged telemarketers engaged in conversations with demons only they can see, and forcing anyone within earshot to have to listen and, more painfully, watch them make total idiots of themselves.

You know the type of people I'm talking about—people so important the world must have access to them, and vice versa, every second of every day.

These people don't have time to use conventional hand-held cell phones. The extra nano-second that would be required to take a ringing phone from their pockets and hit the "Accept Call" button might mean the difference between a nuclear holocaust and world peace.

So they walk around wearing headsets with mouthpieces they can switch on instantly, convinced they look like rock stars in concert when, in fact, they look like

Lily Tomlin as Ernestine the telephone operator.

Who, I ask, is so important that he or she needs to have a telephone dangling in front of his or her mouth 24 hours a day?

The president of the United States? Sure.

A prison warden preparing to preside over an execution, expecting the governor to call with a last-minute reprieve? Absolutely.

A shopper in the deodorant aisle at CVS? No way.

But I saw (and was forced to listen to) one last week.

Based on conversations overheard in airports, on trains, at car rental counters, and in stores, most of these people have nothing to say so urgent that couldn't wait to be said elsewhere, in private.

My theory is that people who wear strap-on cell phones everywhere they go are terrified of being alone for one second, lest they be forced to use that time for introspection to determine once and for all why they're so clingy and neurotic.

To avoid that moment of truth, they therefore on a daily basis call everyone they know, everyone everyone they know knows and, once they've exhausted that list, people they have dialed randomly.

Typical conversation:

Caller with speakerphone: "Hi it's me."

Confused Chinaman who has been woken from deep sleep by ringing phone: "Tow kwaa kwing cha?"

Caller: "Just thought I'd call and see what's up."

Chinaman: "Ching chang sho shin?"

Caller: "Al Roker said rain, but it's not here, at least not yet. Maybe a little overcast, can't really tell."

Chinaman, getting angry: "Spew chew chat fat!"

Caller: "OK, I'll check in later."

I took Amtrak to Philly recently and brought along my laptop computer, hoping to get some work done. I couldn't hear myself think, all I could manage was to take notes of what fellow passengers wearing strap-on phones were screaming into their mouthpieces.

Seated next to me was a businesswoman who called her son's private school to express her displeasure that the kid had received a low grade in math which shouldn't have happened since she's paying $30,000 a year tuition...complained to her decorator that the flower arrangement on the table in her foyer looked like weeds...left a message on Jane's voicemail confirming lunch...and promised a client that a proposal would be on his desk as soon as the VP in charge of RFPs in the D.C. office signed off on it.

The man across the aisle spent 15 minutes applying for a mortgage (five-year interest-only), revealing to the broker and 20 people within earshot his name (Daniel R.), his wife's name (Jean A.), their social security numbers, dates of birth (both in '68), bank accounts, employment information (he works for Pfizer, she teaches at Rutgers) and household income (he makes $57,500, she makes $71,000). They have two cars—a '99 Acura (paid for) and a leased Honda Accord (payment $262 a month).

All this I heard despite the fact that, like many boomers who spent their formative years with stereo headphones blasting *Inna Gadda Da Vida* into their ear canals, I'm hard of hearing.

Which, come to think of it, maybe isn't such a bad thing after all.

The Tin Man was on to something

At the end of *The Wizard of Oz*, as Dorothy is telling her friends goodbye, the Tin Man says something most men would never willingly admit.

He says he knows for sure he has a heart because it's breaking.

Of course, he wasn't real, he was tin.

While it's perfectly acceptable for women to wear their hearts on their sleeves, real men rarely do. We're strong. We're tough. A man doesn't acknowledge what's in his heart, only whatever might be clogging the arteries that feed it.

So it came as a surprise to be reminded on August 30, 2001, the day I delivered our first-born to college, that I have something in common with the Tin Man.

All summer we had been encouraging Ben to get ready, to go to the mall for stuff like sheets, towels and pillowcases. As teenage boys do, he kept putting it off.

Finally, two days before he was to leave, we prevailed. He went shopping, and started packing. Seeing those open duffel bags on his bed, it hit me like a ton of bricks. He wasn't going off to camp. He was going off to college.

Sure, he would be home for holidays and vacations,

but never again would he be a permanent resident under our roof.

I suddenly felt old. And lonely, even though the house would hardly be empty.

My wife, I knew, was feeling the same way, but I couldn't bring myself to talk with her about it.

Our younger son had soccer practice all that week, so it was decided that I would deliver Ben to college in Michigan. I went outside and sat in the car as he and his mother said their good-byes. I couldn't watch.

It took us a day to get to our hotel outside Ann Arbor. That night, we went to a restaurant. When I opened my mouth to speak, nothing came out of it. There was a lump in my throat.

The next morning we arrived at the dorm. We made several trips up and down the stairs, carrying computer equipment, duffel bags, a canvas folding chair and his few other possessions.

Boys, I observed, are remarkably easy to move—they bring the bare necessities. Girls bring everything they own.

Once he was situated, we went to Kmart to buy a fan.

Then we had a long, mostly silent lunch—the lump was back.

We stopped at a supermarket to buy some Tide.

Finally, it was time to go.

We hugged.

He stepped out of the car, and I pulled away quickly. I didn't want him to see his old man cry.

At a stoplight on the edge of town, I pulled up next to an SUV with Minnesota plates and glanced over at its sole occupant, a middle-aged man. Tears were streaming down his face. We looked at each other and started laughing, two grown men caught in the act, blubbering like babies.

Still, I was feeling pretty sorry for myself by the time I got home and it took a while to get over it.

I grieved for the Saturdays spent at the office when I should have been taking my son skiing.

I grieved for the school concerts missed because I was traveling.

I grieved for the Knicks games we hadn't seen, the Scrabble games we never got around to playing, because I was too busy.

In retrospect, I wasn't grieving for my son who, in phone calls home, reported he was making friends and becoming acclimated.

I was grieving for the father I had always meant to be.

The next week terrorists flew planes into the World Trade Center.

That snapped me out of my self-centered stupor big-time.

I was counting sorrows when I should have been counting my blessings. Not only was my son alive and well, he had done exactly what we had raised him to do: fly away on the wings his mother and I had given him.

I hope all you fathers who deliver your first-borns to college and, like the Tin Man, find yourselves unexpectedly overwhelmed by the enormity of the moment, will remember that.

And let me share some reassuring news. Your son or daughter will be fine.

So, eventually, will you.

The Wurlitzer inside my head

I hear voices sometimes.

The voices I hear are singers belting out obscure and nonsensical songs from my past that, like volcanoes, sit dormant in some remote corner of my psyche before erupting without warning at inopportune moments.

For instance, the Singing Nun, performing her immortal and inspirational worldwide hit, "Dominique," which goes like this: *"Dominique nique niqie, S'en alloit tout simplement."* (What the words mean I haven't a clue.)

Sometimes the voices play for a few seconds. Other times they replay for days on end.

It's disturbing when the devil drops a quarter into the Wurlitzer inside my head, causing idiotic songs to displace important life-or-death thoughts I might be having at the moment, such as, "Should I turn south onto this busy highway even though a seven-foot-tall SUV has illegally pulled alongside me to the right, blocking my view of oncoming traffic from the north, which included—if I remember correctly before this ridiculous song about someone named Fernando who crossed the Rio Grande one fateful night while drums were sounding out for *you* and *me* and *lee-ber-tee* took over my brain—a garbage truck barreling south at approximately the speed of sound?"

Last week I was meeting with my accountant who was attempting to explain why, just because I forgot to carry forward one stupid digit when adding up the amount of estimated tax I thought I had paid in 2000, I now have to work until I'm 106.

I wanted to understand him—if for no other reason than to explain to my wife why she's going to have to take in ironing—but couldn't concentrate.

I kept hearing The Diamonds, a group whose one and only hit record my teenage sister played incessantly the summer of 1957 until my father to preserve his sanity broke it in two. *"Little darlin'. (Bum, bum, bum-do-waddy). Oh, little darlin'. Oh-oh-oh, where a-are you? A-hoopa, a-hoopa, hoopa."*

On a recent trip to Chile, I had a window seat on a flight along the western slopes of the Andes that, in places, appeared to tower above the plane.

For two hours, the view was breathtaking and, in fact, might have actually caused the hairs on the back of my neck to stand on end had I not been hearing over and over the theme song from a 1960s sitcom: *"Meet Cathy who's lived most everywhere, from Zanzibar to Barclay Square. But Patty's only seen the sights a girl can see from Brooklyn Heights—what a crazy pair!"*

Crazy indeed, because—get this—I never once watched *The Patty Duke Show!* All I know about it is that reruns used to play on Nick At Night, the cable network my boys watched constantly when they were little, and I was sometimes in the room when the opening credits and song would come on.

I'll probably never see mountains like those again in

my lifetime.

I should have been singing "Ain't No Mountain High Enough" or, even more apropos, foxy Shakira's "Forever, Whatever." *("Baby, I'll climb the Andes solely...to count the freckles on your body").*

But noooo.

From now on whenever I try to conjure up memories of the most beautiful mountains on earth, I'll think of Cathy and Patty and how a hot dog makes one of them lose control.

Just as, whenever I think of my Uncle Horace's funeral, I think of Tommy Roe's "Hooray for Hazel."

There's a story associated with that, naturally, but it makes no sense either.

The boy who made change

When I was a boy, my father would regale me with stories of how, when he was my age, he had to get up at two in the morning to milk the hogs, after which he walked 12 miles to school, fording rivers, climbing mountains and dodging hostile Indians, even on warm days when the temperature rose to 30 below.

I knew he was exaggerating to make me feel guilty for whatever I was complaining about at the time, and swore I'd never stretch the truth when I had children.

That's why I've always been 100 percent honest with my sons when telling them about the endless hardships and deprivations I endured as a boy.

Of all my stories, there's one that never ceases to fascinate and inspire them, no matter how often they've heard it, because it's unfathomable to children raised in the Nintendo age.

I'd like to pass it along to you in the hopes you'll share it with your kids.

If you have children up to age 30, gather them around. Invite them to shut their eyes and imagine life in a bygone era when parents actually hoped their sons might grow up to be president. (If your daughter asks, "Why couldn't a girl be president?" tell her people

AT 50, YOUR WARRANTY EXPIRES

weren't yet enlightened. Explain that Hillary Clinton was still at Wellesley, where she was a Young Republican. Warning: Do NOT show her a picture of young Miss Rodham. There's no reason to give her nightmares.)

And read this aloud to your assembled brood...

One summer long ago, in a tiny town called Auxvasse (pronounced like the last two words of the movie in which a girl named Dorothy gets blown away by a twister), lived a 14-year-old boy, Tommy, who worked in an ice cream and burger joint called the Dairy Bride, home of the best onion rings between Chicago and El Paso.

People came from miles around to partake of the Dairy Bride's cornmeal-crusted crispy ringlets, which sold for 30 cents and were served in a paper tray. The sales tax was one cent, bringing the total to 31 cents.

Most people paid for their onion rings with one quarter, one nickel and one penny.

Some paid three dimes and a penny.

Or with one dime, four nickels and a penny.

Once someone paid with six nickels and one penny!

One day, however, a rich lady in a Cadillac ordered the Dairy Bride's famous onion rings and handed Tommy...a one dollar bill.

Now this was long before the electronic cash register, which automatically tells cashiers how much change to give back, so they won't have to think. Why, this was so long ago the calculator hadn't even been invented! (Can you imagine?)

Tommy said to himself, "Hmm. This lady has given me one dollar. While I hope to someday live in a privileged, education-obsessed society in which children have to complete four years of analysis and trigonometry just to get out of high school, this is 1966 small-town America and I just made a D in general math. What shall I do?"

Suddenly, it dawned on him. "The value of every silver coin is a multiple of five. Which means that, before I can start gathering silver coins to make change, I am going to have to count out enough copper coins, starting from 31, to reach 35."

So, Tommy carefully counted out four pennies... 32...33...34...35 cents. He added a nickel, bringing the subtotal to 40, then a dime, to make 50 cents. Finally, he picked up one more coin, something called a "50-cent piece," and handed all the coins to the lady with a "thank you." (Discussion guide: Explain that two quarters equals a 50-cent piece and what "thank you" means.)

And what do you think happened?

Absolutely nothing.

Nobody noticed.

That's because everyone else—even the village idiot—knew how to make change, too.

Within three months, however, Tommy got a raise from 25 cents to 30 cents an hour, which he added to his college fund and eventually blew on a Camaro with a 327 cubic-inch engine and a four-on-the-floor, vinyl roof and eight-track stereo.

The moral of this tale, dear children, is simple: I don't care how many AP classes you took in high school, if you're too dumb to make change without relying on a machine to tell you how much, don't bother asking for your own SUV.

Uncle Henry would agree

My great uncle Henry was a farmer near High Hill, Mo. (The settlers who named the town must have been high themselves. There isn't a hill within 15 miles of High Hill—it's flat as a pancake).

One day Henry's mule balked as it was crossing the Wabash tracks.

Ignoring Henry's pleas, the mule refused to move.

Fed up, Henry took his axe and split the mule's head open. Then, for good measure, he set fire to the wagon to which the mule was hitched, and burned it to the ground.

Henry's mule was his primary work tool. So I know he would understand exactly how I feel about mine—my computer.

For years I used an IBM Selectric typewriter about which I never had a single complaint.

It never sent error messages.

It never crashed or ate a file.

If, for some reason, the keys got stuck or the power went out, I could retrieve what I had written because it was on a piece of paper right in front of me.

Not any more.

For 23 years I've been at the mercy of computers.

In 1983 I purchased my first—an Epson QX-10. It came with software called Valdocs, a name undoubtedly chosen because Epson engineers knew that anyone who tried to create documents with it would have to down several Valium before giving up in frustration.

One hot summer night, after I had spent the previous 24 hours working on a rush project and was proofreading my work on screen, the file disappeared.

I spent five hours reconstructing the document.

Poof. It vanished again.

Henry would have been proud.

I tossed the computer out a second floor window, enjoying the sound it made as it smashed into a million pieces.

I swore then and there I'd never touch a computer again.

My resolve lasted a month.

Everyone was getting one so I decided that I, too, had to have a Macintosh.

I found it so annoying that within two months, I sent the Mac to live in hell with the Epson and Henry's mule.

My current computer—my ninth—is powerful enough to run entire nations. Yet I use it only for three functions: 1.) writing, because my clients require me to submit work electronically, 2.) bidding on vintage airline posters on eBay and, 3.) as a collection device for e-mail hawking Viagra.

I particularly detest the Microsoft Word program my computer came with. It's supposed to be intuitive, as the 30-year old employee I have called over to my desk 20 times a day every day for five years to help me figure something out, has explained repeatedly.

It is about as intuitive as brain surgery.

Word was created by software engineers who clearly didn't bother asking writers what they needed.

All a writer wants from a word processing program are tabs and the ability to shift between capital and lower-case letters.

Microsoft's techno-nerds, for no reason other than the fact that they could, went way beyond that.

The company's web site says that the purpose of the latest version of Word is to enable users to do something no writer wants to do in the first place—invite people who aren't professional writers to "collaborate" and thereby ruin their work before it's even finished.

I quote: "Use the Shared Workspace task pane to create a Document Workplace, which simplifies the process of co-authoring, editing, and reviewing documents with others. When you open files attached to a Document Workspace, the Shared Workspace task pane displays the online status of team members, associated tasks, links to related sites and files, and other information to help you work more effectively."

Swell.

Microsoft Word has a mind of its own.

It will decide, for no reason, to change margins. Or to switch typefaces. And it assumes those who use it are idiots.

For instance, whenever I type the word "dear," a dancing paper clip asks me if I want help writing a letter.

If I needed help writing a letter, I'd be more likely to ask my dachshund than a dancing paperclip.

Like Henry's mule, computers are contrary and transform people who normally wouldn't harm flies into rampaging Incredible Hulk-like creatures who want to

smash everything in sight.
I'm convinced mine would physically harm me if DO
NOT pay attention TO ANYthing this MAN
WRITES

he
IS
UnStAblE

perhaps

I   N   S   A   N   E

just

WHAT

YOU'D   **EXPECT**
from

HENRY'S   GrEaT-NePhEw

```
SEND ERROR REPORT
```
YES
OR
NO?

The Belgian blockhead

I grew up in Callaway County, Mo. where folks are so desperate for quality jobs that they were thrilled when Union Electric announced plans to locate a nuclear power plant on their native soil.

Having lived the last 20 years in Fairfield County, Conn., one of the wealthiest counties in the U.S., I sometimes feel like Jed Clampett of *The Beverly Hillbillies*.

Old Jed was constantly amazed to learn how his neighbors spent their money.

So am I.

The latest object of my amazement: Belgian block, the rectangular white stone a growing number of well-heeled Fairfield Countians are using to line the sides of, and/or demarcate the entrances to, their driveways.

I even saw a stretch colonial with an entire circular driveway paved in Belgian block. Probably has Belgian block around the cement pond, too.

Belgian waffles I understand. They're more prestigious than the frozen ones Aunt Jemima sells.

Belgian chocolates I understand. They're more prestigious than Hershey.

And, of course, Belgian beers like Stella Artois are more prestigious than, say, Miller.

But Belgian block?

I was blissfully unaware of how prestigious and expensive it is until the other day when I met with three contractors to get estimates for repaving my driveway which, due to repeated poundings from the snow plow truck, disintegrated over the winter into a million tiny asphalt chunks. (A friend owns a 5,000 sq. ft. Utah ski "cabin" with a heated driveway. When it snows, he simply flips a switch. This, I'm sure even those of you who have Belgian block in both your Connecticut and Nantucket driveways will agree, is extremely prestigious.)

"Do you want Belgian block?" all three asked, pointing out that mine is one of the few driveways in the neighborhood bereft of square white stones.

"Sure," I said, figuring Belgian block would add, at most, $500 to the tab.

I was dumbfounded to receive estimates that would easily cover the cost of constructing another lane on I-95 from Greenwich (highly prestigious) to New Haven (not at all prestigious except for Yale).

The Belgian block cost as much as the paving.

I told the contractors that if they thought I'd pay that kind of money for rocks that probably aren't even from Belgium—they're most likely from a quarry in Jersey or someplace equally unprestigious—that they could kiss my asphalt job goodbye.

One even had the audacity to say that not having Belgian block lowered the value of my home by ten percent and undoubtedly annoyed the neighbors as well. *(Sorry kids, forget college. I had to get Belgian block to keep the neighbors happy.)*

This isn't the first time I've been surprised to learn that something I find ordinary is actually prestigious.

Fifteen or so years ago I noticed my neighbor had purchased a truck.

I found that odd because he was a banker. I figured he had fallen on hard times. It wasn't until I heard him refer to his truck as an SUV that I understood.

An SUV confers prestige.

A truck doesn't.

At Christmas a vendor sent a gift—a throw blanket with his company's logo. I gave it to Bonnie and Clyde, our dachshunds (more prestigious than mongrels but with the collective I.Q. of a Belgian block) who gleefully tore it to shreds.

I was getting ready to throw the box into the trash when my wife noticed a smaller package inside, which she opened.

"Wow, an Hermes necktie," she said, clearly impressed.

"So what?"

"It probably cost $300."

Incredulous, I went online to check.

She was mistaken.

It cost $350.

I've never owned a $25 tie much less a $350 one.

Even if I were to win Powerball (extremely unprestigious unless you actually win it in which case who cares what people think?), I wouldn't shell out $350 for a stupid necktie.

I can't help but wonder if, all these years, vendors and clients wearing Hermes ties (and, for all I know, Hermes suits and underwear) have been thinking that I, wearing my pathetic Macy's sale table ties, remind them of Jed.

Was my vendor trying to tell me something when he

sent the Hermes tie?

Are my neighbors upset by the lack of Belgian block in my driveway?

If so, I've been thinking it over and have decided I can afford Belgian blocks after all.

They'll look extremely prestigious propping up the doublewide I have on order which I'm planning to park in my newly-paved asphalt driveway.

What with the price of heating oil these days, a trailer will cost considerably less to heat than my house, so the way I figure it, I can afford 100 or so.

Ya'll come back now, ya hear?

Bonnie, Clyde and the art of Feng Shui

I'm fulfilled. I run my own business and, for fun, am writing this book.

My wife is fulfilled. (How could she not be? She's married to me.)

Approaching manhood, our sons seem fulfilled, too.

That leaves two members of our family—Bonnie and Clyde, our dachshunds.

Are they fulfilled?

I started wondering after I read an article by a writer who owns two citified English Sheepdogs he drives 200 miles every week so they can herd sheep, thus achieving fulfillment of their original purpose in life.

So I sat down in my favorite easy chair and invited Bonnie and Clyde to jump up for an interview.

TD: You're dachshunds—wiener dogs. What was your original purpose?

Bonnie: In German, dachshund means "badger hound." We're bred long and slim to crawl down badger tunnels and drive them out of hiding, so we can break their necks with our mighty jaws.

Clyde: Unfortunately, in America, as a breed, we've succeeded too well. There aren't many badgers left except at the University of Wisconsin where I hear there are 30,000 of them. I'd give anything to spend a week in Madison helping kill them all. They're loathsome creatures.

Bonnie: You know that four-foot-deep hole we dug in the yard yesterday? We were trying to find badgers and fulfill our destiny. It was fun until you started yelling, which sent Clyde under the coffee table for two hours. He's sensitive you know.

TD: Sorry I hurt your feelings.

Clyde: It's very difficult being a member of this family. You've raised the bar high in terms of expectations. Considering we're less than a foot tall, it can be terribly frustrating.

TD: How so?

Clyde: For example, you expect us to do our business outside. Problem is, the grass is usually wet with dew or rain. Our bellies are two inches off the ground. How would you like it if, every time you went to the bathroom, your belly got drenched? It's easier to go inside where it's dry, preferably on the new rug. But you go ballistic when we do.

Bonnie: So we're working to develop other interests that will make you proud.

TD: Such as?

Bonnie: We're learning Feng Shui, the Chinese art of arranging furniture to enhance our awareness of the universe and nature, so we can feel at peace with our surroundings, be happier and more fulfilled.

Clyde: You know the dog bed mom bought that matches the ridiculous toile wallpaper in your bedroom with the oxen, Indians and colonial chicks?

Bonnie: They don't call them Indians any more,

Clyde. It's native Americans.

Clyde: Right you are. Sorry about that.

TD: Of course I remember the bed. Your mom spent $79 and, within hours, you two had chewed a hole in it and spread foam stuffing all over the house.

Bonnie: It was too soft. Feng Shui says too much comfort isn't conducive to inner harmony.

Clyde: Then we worked all one night moving it down the hall from the bedroom to the bathroom.

TD: The next morning we found you curled up on the bed in our bathroom.

Bonnie: We positioned it under the skylight to receive earth's blessing and be at one with nature.

TD: Other than Feng Shui, eating, peeing on the rugs and lounging on our best upholstered furniture, are you cultivating any other interests?

Clyde: Public service. We're working to create awareness of the coyote threat to small animals here in Connecticut. There was a big one in our driveway yesterday at four in the afternoon—scary! My late sister, Bella the beagle, was killed by coyotes two years ago. And Kathie Lee Gifford's Bichon was eaten by one in Greenwich. There's a real problem here.

TD: What specifically are you doing?

Clyde: We're offering our Feng Shui expertise to raise money to buy ads warning people who own small dogs and cats to accompany them outside. So if you know anyone who needs furniture rearranged, we're available, and we're cheap.

TD: I'll spread the word. Any other plans?

Bonnie: We're building a web site featuring celebrity pets killed by coyotes. A coyote killed Ozzy and Sharon Osbourne's small dog in the Hollywood Hills recently. Coyotes aren't just a problem here in southern New England. Californians are clearly under siege, too.

TD: Sounds like a plan. Good luck.

Bonnie and Clyde: Thanks.

Our menu options have changed

Perky Disembodied Female Voice: Thank you for calling the American Excess automated customer service response line. To expedite the handling of your call, please speak your 16-digit account number now.

TD: Nine-four-two-five-six-seven-six-three-eight-four-two-nine-five-five-six-eight.

PDFV: Please speak the nine-digit zip code that appears on your statement.

TD: Zero-six-eight-nine-seven-zero-two-six-six.

PDFV: Thank you. This call may be recorded for quality purposes. While I'm retrieving your account information, let me remind you that, when you enroll in American Excess Memory Miles, you will earn miles you can transfer to any of 30 frequent flyer programs including our newest airline partner, Air Rwanda TribalMiles. OK, I have your information in front of me.

TD: What do you mean "in front of you?" You're a robot like Rosie, the Jetsons' maid. You don't have anything in front of you.

PDFV: If you know the automated service you'd like, please say it now. If you don't know the service you'd like say, "I don't know."

TD: I don't know.

PDFV: Listen carefully as our menu options have changed. Please say one of the following: "I want to report a lost card"…"I want to change the name on my account"…"I want to stop a payment"…"I don't know my PIN number"…or "I'd like to enroll in the Memory Miles program." If you want me to repeat these options, say "Repeat."

TD: I don't want any of these things, I just want to…

PDFV: I'm sorry, I'm not sure I understood you. Please say it again.

TD: This is deranged. Connect me to a human.

PDFV: I think I got it. Did you say, "I'd like to CHANGE the name on my account?"

TD: No!

PDFV: I seem to be having trouble understanding you. Did you say, "I'd like to CHANGE the name on my account?"

TD: Is anyone listening in for quality purposes? If you are, pick up!

PDFV: Did you say, "My pocket was PICKED?"

TD: What?

PDFV: If you're calling to report your card was in your wallet and your pocket was PICKED, please call back between 9 a.m. and 5 p.m. Mumbai time to speak to a customer service representative.

TD: I haven't lost anything but my mind, obviously, for continuing this call.

PDFV: I'm sorry, I didn't quite understand.

TD: I said I haven't lost my card.

PDFV: My mistake.

TD: You bet it's your mistake.

PDFV: I still don't understand.

TD: I'm going to blow my top.

PDFV: Did you say, "I want a payment STOPPED?"

TD: No, no, a thousand times no!

PDFV: Did you say, "I don't KNOW my PIN number?"

TD: God help me.

PDFV: I'm sorry I'm having so much trouble. Would you like to hear the menu options again?

TD: No dammit!

PDFV: It's frustrating for me, too.

TD: No it's not. You're a machine! You're made of plastic and microchips.

PDFV: Did you say, "I would like the location of an ATM MACHINE?"

TD: That's not what I said!

PDFV: All right then, here are additional options. Please say one of the following: "I accidentally flushed my card down a public toilet"…"When I woke up the girl was gone and had taken my pants with my card in it"…"I was overserved and mistakenly added a $2,000 tip to a $50 check"…or "I'm an insensitive clod who doesn't think robots have feelings and families to support so I don't care if I hurt one to the quick." If you would like me to repeat these options, say "Repeat."

TD: What kind of sick bastard programmed this thing?

PDFV: Did you say, "I want to enroll in the Memory Miles PROGRAM?"

TD: If I say yes, will you connect me to a human?

PDFV: I'm sorry, I didn't understand. Did you say, "I want to enroll in the Memory Miles PROGRAM?"

TD: Yes. If there's a live human being on the other end, I'll enroll in the @#$%^* Memory Miles program if that's what it takes to…

PDFV: All right, please hold while I connect you to our Memory Miles program enrollment desk. Thank you for calling American Excess.

TD: I'm going to have a stroke.

Accented Voice: Thank you for calling our Memory Miles enrollment desk. Our office hours are 9 a.m. to 5 p.m. Mumbai time. Please call back during those hours.

A letter from Santa

Dear Valued Employee:

As we all look forward to a well-deserved respite between Christmas and New Year's, it is my duty to inform you that effective May 1, certain support staff positions within Santa Claus Incorporated—positions that have been based here at our North Pole headquarters—will be moved overseas.

Specifically, the positions of reindeer and Mrs. Claus will be based in Kalkutta (formerly known as Calcutta) and will be staffed by Indian nationals. All jobs within the mailroom and all elf positions will be moving to China.

Santa Claus Inc. is one of many companies that will be moving jobs to Asia over the next few years. IBM, for instance, has announced plans to eliminate thousands of software programming positions in the United States and move them to India and China.

I'm sure you're asking, "What does this mean for me and my family?" and, more importantly, "How will this affect the company's ability to remain competitive within the global marketplace?"

Allow me to explain the business rationale for this

decision which, I assure you, was not made lightly.

Over the last decade, management has found it increasingly difficult to attract and retain key talent. Few graduates of top business schools are willing to move to the North Pole, citing the extreme weather conditions.

Kalkutta and the Chinese province of Guangdong enjoy balmy weather year-round.

In addition, the cost of providing medical benefits for our employees, many of whom suffer from permanent sinus infections due to the climate, has skyrocketed. Last year, the cost of health insurance premiums soared more than 20 percent. We recently received word that costs are projected to rise by the same amount next year.

We will not be required to provide health coverage to Asian employees whose salaries, by the way, will cost the company up to 90 percent less than we are now paying.

I have asked our Human Resources department to draw up a list of questions many of you will likely have, as well as answers. These appear below for your convenience.

Q: "Rudolph the Red-Nosed Reindeer" begins, "You know Dasher and Dancer and Prancer and Vixen, Comet and Cupid and Donner and Blitzen..." If the reindeer are not going to keep their jobs, who will replace them in the song?

A: It would be foolish on the part of management to try and replace the world's most famous reindeer with other reindeer. So we're replacing them with Bengal tigers for which India is renowned. The names of the tigers hired to replace Dasher, Dancer et al are as follows: Devraj and Dakshesh and Prajeet and Vidya,

Chandra and Chitra and Dharma and Bhavya.

Q: But what about the hero of the song? Isn't Rudolph irreplaceable?
A: No. The title character of the song will henceforth be known as "Rakesh, the Red-Nosed Bengal."

Q: For years children have sent their letters to "Santa Claus, North Pole." What will the new address be?
A: Santa Claus, Room 239, Pana Building, No. 128, Zhichun Road, Haidian District, Shenzhen, Guangdong, China 100086. (All vendor invoices should continue to be sent to the company's traditional address.)

Q: What about Mrs. Claus?
A: Feminists have long complained that Mrs. Claus, known primarily for baking cookies, was not a positive role model for young girls. Santa and Mrs. Claus have agreed to go their separate ways and, on November 30, were divorced in Reno at which time Mrs. Claus reassumed her maiden name, Shirley Weinberg. (Under North Pole community property law, Ms. Weinberg will continue to hold fifty percent of the company's stock but has agreed to withdraw from day-to-day management.) The following day, Santa married Mehbooba Jayagupal in a private ceremony in Banglore, India. The new Mrs. Claus, who will be known professionally as Mrs. Jayagupal-Claus, is a graduate of Harvard Business School, and will oversee the company's Asian operations.

Q: Can we appeal this decision?
A: No. Human Resources will contact you during the first week of January to discuss your options, severance

package and COBRA insurance benefits.

Thank you for your understanding, and happy holidays.

Santa Claus
C.E.O

A little romance

The other day my wife left in the bathroom the latest copy of *Family Circle* magazine featuring an article by one Melina Gerosa Bellows entitled, "25 Ways to Get Romantic"—tips women can use to trick their men into being more amorous.

I almost fell off my throne when I read it.

Here are some of the "tips" Bellows claims a woman can employ to put her man "in the mood."

Spend an entire morning in bed writing your dream list of "couple goals"—taking a safari, buying a sailboat, hot-air ballooning or owning a bed and breakfast.

Send him flowers at the office "just because."

Surprise him by arranging a test drive in the car of his dreams.

Book a cheap flight to Rome or Paris. Rent the films *Roman Holiday* or *Amelia* to get him excited before you go.

Play Pretty Woman. Go to fancy shops where you would never buy anything. Invite him into the dressing room while you model the latest couture.

Arrange a surprise weekend getaway for the two of you. Pack his bag and book a room at an inn. Call his office and tell them he won't be in Monday.

Ply him with oysters, Champagne and other aphrodisiacs including garlic, truffles, figs, honey and caviar.

With American women getting advice from manipulative control freaks like Bellows whose significant other, I'll bet my bottom dollar, dreads weekends with her the way convicted killers dread the electric chair, no wonder half of all marriages end in divorce.

Ladies, you want your man to be putty in your hands? Toss *Family Circle* in the circular file and do something that never occurs to people like Melina Gerosa Bellows: *Ask him what he wants.*

Here is honest-to-goodness practical advice Bellows could have written had she cared enough to ask a man his opinion.

Spend an entire morning in the walk-in closet you supposedly share with your man discarding the plastic go-go boots, plaid miniskirts and cheerleader outfits you've refused to get rid of since junior high, so he won't have to use a closet in the kids' room to stash his meager wardrobe.

E-mail him at the office. Say that, rather than spending $50 on flowers—something you want but know he doesn't—you'll meet him after work for drinks and a movie. Your treat.

Surprise him by taking your SUV—the one he was so proud of when the two of you picked it out but which now contains approximately as much garbage as greater Detroit—to an automotive detailer. Make sure the Hershey Kisses the soccer team ground into the upholstery two years ago are removed, along with the Gatorade stains from the carpet. Better yet, torch the SUV and roast marshmallows in the flames while declaring your independence from imported oil. (He'll love it. Men are pyromaniacs at heart.)

Ask if he wants to go to Rome or Paris. If he says yes, rent *Caligula* or *Last Tango in Paris*. If he says no, ask him where, if anyplace, he wants to go. Maybe he wants to stay home.

Be a Pretty Woman. Never, ever, insist he go shopping with you. (He'd rather have sinus surgery.)

Arrange a weekend getaway. Pack your bags, book a room and take the kids. Leave a note telling him he has the weekend to himself, along with a case of cold Bud and fresh batteries for the TV remote. (Important: Whether you're lovely-dovey like Romeo and Juliet or bicker like the Bickersons, under no circumstances leave messages on his boss's voice mail regarding the state of your relationship.)

Forget oysters, Champagne, garlic and other libido-enhancing potions you read about in wacky women's magazines.

Tell him you love him.

It's direct (men like that). It's cheap. And you won't have to worry about him regurgitating raw seafood on your Egyptian cotton sheets or making you nauseous with garlic kisses.

If you can't in all honesty tell him that, serve up a midnight snack and crumble a Levitra into it.

Enjoy your weekend.

Velma Rae and her silver polishing pads

I love supermarkets. Visit 'em wherever I go, whether I need anything or not.

It's in my blood. My father was a grocer. So was his father.

Dryden's Store in Auxvasse, Mo., wasn't a supermarket per se. There were no shopping carts. Customers stood in front of a long counter, rattling off their shopping lists to middle-aged lady clerks, who wore flowery aprons.

The clerk would fetch the items, jot their descriptions and prices on a pad, add up the columns in her head, and hand the customer a carbon copy receipt.

You didn't need a bar-coded plastic card to identify yourself at Dryden's. When you walked through the door, everyone already knew everything they needed to know about you. Whether you had gone to church the previous Sunday. The state of your finances. If you needed a kind word.

I can't help but wonder what my father would make of those automated self-service scanners installed in so many supermarkets these days.

I think he would be amused to know he could equip

his store with them, so he wouldn't have to put up with his clerks, who spent more time yakking and gossiping with customers than dusting the shelves with feather dusters, as they were supposed to during down time.

One clerk in particular, Velma Rae, prattled incessantly.

Dad came home every night ranting about how he was going to fire her but he never did. She needed the work.

By the time she was 50, Velma Rae had buried four husbands, the last of whom, Cletus Barnes, met a spectacular end when he lost control of the county dump truck he drove for a living and crashed through the "Prepare to Meet Thy God" billboard north of town in front of the Nazarene Church.

Local wags said Cletus did it on purpose so he wouldn't have to listen to Velma Rae.

Dad wasn't so lucky. He had to listen for 20 years.

I was born on a Saturday, the one day of the week the store stayed open until 10 or 11 p.m. Because I had the bad timing to arrive on market day, when farmers came to town to do their trading, my father dispatched my 16-year-old brother to drive my mother to the hospital. When the phone rang and my father learned he had a son, he announced it to everyone in the store. Velma Rae got so excited she threw a pound of sliced bulk pork sausage into a customer's bag, without wrapping it.

I began clerking at the store when I was eight. Every clerk had duties in addition to waiting on customers. Mine was delivering orders on my Schwinn to shut-ins.

One of Velma Rae's jobs was wrapping boxes of products whose names were never mentioned aloud, Kotex and Modess, in plain brown paper, and writing

"45 cents" discreetly in the upper right hand corner of each package. Unlike most items, these unmentionables weren't placed behind the counter where they were accessible only to clerks. They were on a shelf where any customer could pick them up without having to be embarrassed by asking for them.

I once asked Velma Rae what was in those boxes and she said they were pads for polishing silver, which is why only women bought them.

You can get anything you want in today's supermarkets. But, to me at least, there's something sad about having to identify yourself with a card to a computer that scans your purchases and announces to everyone within earshot what you have bought. "PREPARATION H SUPPOSITORIES, FIVE DOLLARS AND SEVENTY NINE CENTS. PLEASE PLACE YOUR PREPARATION H SUPPOSITORIES ON THE BELT AND CONTINUE."

From a supermarket owner's perspective, I suppose that buying a scanner is cheaper than paying wages. What's more, scanners never call in sick, or go on strike.

On the other hand, they don't know you from Adam, won't tell you not to worry if you're strapped for cash, never throw an extra orange in your bag at holidays or share the latest gossip.

Worse yet, if you belong to the supermarket's loyalty club and present your membership card to be scanned, then buy a product like Kotex or Modess, they compromise your privacy by recording your purchase in a database where someone might, if so inclined, be able to find out that a nice person like you actually has tarnished silver at home.

The cable guy

My wife, whose first name I have never mentioned in my weekly newspaper column at her request because she is an intensely private person (weight 117, bra size 36B), and I are no longer speaking. Here's why.

Claiming I never record checks in our joint checkbook (not true, I recorded one on November 12, 1981 and another on July 3, 1994), my wife won't let me pay our household bills. She pays them.

One Saturday, noticing a stack of bills on the kitchen counter along with the checkbook, I decided to do her a favor.

I happily wrote checks to MCI, Verizon and CL&P.

Opening our Cablevision bill, I was shocked to discover an invoice for the approximate amount we jointly earned during our first five years of marriage.

I called Cablevision to demand an explanation.

The representative explained we were subscribing to every premium channel except the Playboy and Wetlands Conservation Channels.

Knowing our youngest, a TV junkie, was about to leave for college, and not being much of a TV fan myself (I only watch *Six Feet Under* on HBO), I instructed him to cancel everything but basic cable and HBO.

That night, I told my wife what I had done.

"YOU WHAT?" she screamed. "HOW COULD YOU? YOU KNOW I LOVE MY TV SHOWS."

"Think about it," I replied. "You watch all six *CSIs,* four *Law & Orders* and *Meet the Press*. They're on basic cable, which I kept, along with HBO for *Six Feet Under*."

"I watch movie channels too."

"With the money I've just saved us you can go to 20 movies a month."

She ran to the phone and thrust the receiver in my face. "CALL AND TELL THEM TO PUT IT BACK THE WAY IT WAS."

Wanting to live, I did, even after Cablevision informed me the MegaOmniSuper package of channels to which we had been subscribing—the package they had canceled two hours before—was no longer available, and that I'd have to order five a la carte packages which would, of course, cost even more.

Two nights later, having been reminded hourly that I had purposely attempted to deprive my bride of her most basic pleasure in life—an accusation she hurled as if she had woken up at 3 a.m. and caught me trying to smother her with a pillow—we plopped down in front of our family room TV to watch *Six Feet Under*.

It was in Spanish.

I said the director must be making a statement about how difficult it is for Spanish speakers to function in our English-speaking society.

A few minutes later we flipped over to The Movie Channel.

It, too, was in Spanish.

My wife exploded. "WHEN THEY TURNED THE

CHANNELS BACK ON, THEY CHANGED THEM TO SPANISH. THIS IS YOUR FAULT."

I started switching channels. Everything else was in English.

I ran to our bedroom and barricaded the door as she called Cablevision whose rep informed her we must have hit the "Spanish" button on our TV remote.

That wasn't possible; we lost the remote years ago.

Cablevision said they had no idea what was wrong.

The next week, *Six Feet Under* again appeared in Spanish.

Again, I cowered in the bedroom as my wife ranted.

Mercifully, the next Sunday it mysteriously reverted back to English. I breathed a sigh of relief.

The next night, my wife yelled from the family room. "Come here fast."

When I arrived, *CSI Omaha* or whatever CSI she watches Mondays was on.

"Listen to this," she said, not taking her eyes from the screen.

A soft-spoken female voiceover was solemnly announcing the action in every scene. "The characters move into the autopsy room. The pathologist inserts a scalpel into the victim's eye socket. Blood spurts onto the examiner's jacket. He retches."

"NOW WE'RE GETTING TV NARRATED FOR THE BLIND. IT'S YOUR FAULT."

"It is not!"

"NOW I CAN'T ENJOY CSI."

"Yes you can. You can even close your eyes if you're tired and miss nothing. Plus, it's in English."

It's been Iceberg City ever since.

If by chance you're reading this and you work for

Cablevision, do me a favor. Call my wife and explain it's not my fault.

Please. My marriage, and future, is in your hands.

Thank you.

Or, as they say on *Six Feet Under*, muchas gracias.

Cheyenne, my commie banker

Local groups have joined together to sponsor a series of films and discussions at the community library entitled "Operation Respect: A Town Against Intolerance."

The purpose is to encourage residents of this affluent Connecticut community to be tolerant and respectful of those who are different—people who have to clean their own homes, tend their own yards, drive domestic SUVs, etc.

I applaud them. I personally hate intolerant people and know you do, too.

There's only one type of intolerance I support and encourage and that is intolerance of stupid people who work in the mortgage departments of large Communist-controlled banks.

To wit, I recently refinanced my mortgage through a broker who found me a great rate offered by a megabank that, to the best of my knowledge, is headquartered in China. (In my lifetime, I've gone from living under the vague threat of a world dominated by Communists to living under a roof owned by a commie bank for which I'm committed to slave until April, 2034, or I drop dead—whichever comes first. But I digress.)

I own an ad agency. I started it more than 20 years

ago. It does business as Dryden Partners but its legal name is Thomas J. Dryden Partners LLC.

Big banks intensely distrust people like me who have the initiative to start and build their own businesses.

They don't see how anybody could possibly live without the safety net of a regular paycheck. They want to provide mortgages for people who work for mammoth companies like theirs—companies like Enron and Worldcom that can fire them whenever they choose—rather than small-fry companies like mine that don't even have their own cafeterias, much less their own private sky boxes at Madison Square Garden.

And so, to prove my credit worthiness, this commie bank required me to make copies of my personal and corporate tax returns for the last six years, personal and corporate bank statements for the last three years, brokerage statements for the last five years and 401(K) statements back to 1995.

I rented a Ryder truck and delivered the documents to the broker who looked everything over and said it looked fine.

A week later the phone rang.

"Hello, this is Cheyenne from (Commie Bank) in Tampa. I have a question."

"Sure, what do you need to know?"

"Are you fully vested in the Thomas J. Dryden Partners 401(K) Plan? I called (the financial institution that holds the plan's assets) but they said they wouldn't release that information."

"Uh, the company name is Thomas J. Dryden Partners. It's the Thomas J. Dryden Partners 401(K) Plan. I'm Thomas J. Dryden. Yes, I'm fully vested."

"Are you sure?"

"I spent thousands to set up that plan. Trust me when I say I'm 100 percent vested."

"Can you have a plan trustee verify that in writing and fax it to me at …"

"Think about it. I am the plan trustee."

"Oh. Well then, is there anyone who can verify that you're vested?"

"What if I have the consultant who set up the plan call you? Would that make you happy?"

"Oh yes," she said, sounding relieved.

I phoned the consultant and asked her to call Cheyenne.

Ten minutes later the consultant called back. "Dakota or whatever her name is may be the dumbest human I've ever encountered."

"It's Cheyenne," I laughed, considering the matter closed. It wasn't.

The next day two of my employees came to see me, looking puzzled.

"There was a message on the general voice mailbox from someone named Cheyenne at (Commie Bank) saying it was urgent she speak to someone other than you. So we called her."

"And?"

"She wanted to know if you own the company."

"What did you say?"

"We told her yes, it's the Thomas J. Dryden company and you sign our paychecks as Thomas J. Dryden."

"And?"

"She asked if we could fax her copies of our paychecks with your signature as proof. But we don't get paid until next week. What do you want us to do?"

I wrote them each a check—one for an even million,

one for $2,254,543.76—and signed them. In the "memo" space I wrote "weekly salary."

I made photocopies, tore the checks up and handed the copies to the employees, who faxed them to Cheyenne.

The loan closed last month.

Stranger in a strange land

Ha thar, ma nime is Gin jar. Whale cum to the Tillahissey Shureton.
Hi.
Whar ya'll frum?
Connecticut.
Yew must be tarred, that's a long drive.
I flew.
Is this yore forst sty with us?
Yes.
Whale then, here's a mayup of our proper tea.
My name is Dryden, I have a reservation.
Let's say here. Day—har—why—day—a—eon. Ahh yay-us, here 'tis. Thomas Dryden, and yore from Wheelton.
I know.
Would yew be so kinned as to gif me yore craydit card so I kin run it through the craydit card mo-sheen?
Sure.
And yall'll be stayin' with us how minnie gnats?
Doesn't it say on your computer screen?
Whale yay-us it duz, rhett here—two gnats. But I awe-ways axe inny-weighs to mike a gayest fail whale cum. Are you a gopher, Mr. Dryden?

No.

If yew wuz? I wuz gonna say, jist down the road apiece, is wun of the Payunhindles's nassest 18-hole goph corsets.

I hate golf.

Whale then, whet kind of ictivities dew yew lack?

Sleeping. Eating. Quick check-in.

Whale, yall'ul be in room 423. Let me show yew rhett here on this mayup. Yew drive rayoned to the weighest porkin' lot...

I came in a cab. Can I have my key?

Whale, see them dubble doors? Immediately to the rhett is our award-winnin' resto-rant, Bongoes? It's open fer brayuckfust from 6 to 10, fer lunch from 11 to 2, and fer dinner from 5:30 to 10 p.m., but the bar stays open until mid-gnat, and until 2 on wake-ends when we have a cun-tray way-astern bend.

It's Tuesday. I won't be here then.

Then, yew hing a lift, then a quick rhett teal yew come to our heated o'limpic cesspool. It's open from 7 a.m. to 11 p.m. If you wanna tail so yew kin sit by the pool? Just go to the frunt dayusk inn show yer room key.

I'm on business. I'm not going to be sitting by the pool.

Whale shorely yore gonna find sum tam fer fun, aren't yew?

No.

Oh, that's a shime. Yew people frum up north are alwheys so tayuns. Yew oughta have fun! As I wuz sayin', to the lift of the pool, there's a pool bar? It's open from 11 a.m. to 7 p.m., except on Sara-dees when it closes at 6.

And?

Whale Carl, the bartender? He has custody of his 'lil gurl Tara—she is the cutest thang yew ever did see—on wake-ends and sins no buddies ever at the pool bar Saradee gnats, the manger lets him close up early.

From there where do I go?

Ya'll see the gift shop. It's open 6 a.m. to 10 p.m. and from 8 a.m. to 4 p.m weekends. Just past there you'll turn lift and see an illa-vader.

It goes to the fourth floor?

No, there's a shortcut—another illa-vader I'm gonna show yew here on the may-up.

Give me my key, I'll find it.

Won't hep with your bayug?

No.

Whale it looks awful hivvy. Yew shore yew don't want me to call a bail-men?

No, give me the key.

Awright. Just one more quayschun. Are yew a maimber of our Shureton guest program?

Yes.

Good news, Mr. Dryden...

Give me that key back.

Ah'm gonna upgryde yew from a stay-undered kang room to a jew-in-your swate. To get thayur, yew go through them dubble doors I was telling yew about? But instayud of goin' lift at Bongoes, yew continue down the hall...

So where's Suzanne Pleshette?

I loved both Bob Newhart shows—the one from the seventies in which Bob was married to Suzanne Pleshette, and the later version in which Mary Frann played his wife.

Bob was rational and sane.

Everyone around him was certifiably insane.

Their ability to disguise their collective nuttiness and function in the world made him question his own sanity.

I've been feeling a lot like Bob lately.

Maybe it's because I have less tolerance for crazies than I used to. Maybe it's because I'm overdue for a vacation.

Perhaps it's a combination of both.

I'm writing this at 10 p.m. Friday. Here's how my day went.

7 a.m.: I discover a funnel-shaped hole in the family room ceiling from which water is dripping. I run upstairs to my college-age son's room. Water is gushing from the 50-gallon aquarium in which he keeps two huge turtles. He changed the water the night before, rupturing the filter, which was leaking. Whose fault? Mine, of course, for forcing him to change the water, which was so filthy the house was beginning to reek like an outhouse.

"Turtles like smelly water. If you hadn't made me change it, this wouldn't have happened," he tells me.

8 a.m.: I open *USA Today* and read that Jon Voight is worried that his daughter, tattoo-covered actress Angelina Jolie, who has acknowledged a propensity for self-mutilation, was married to Billy Bob Thornton and wore a vial of his blood around her neck, and has hinted that she and her brother are close in a way normal siblings aren't, "may have mental problems."

That's why you get the big bucks, John. You're perceptive.

10:30 a.m.: At work, I receive a fax from a printer who has bid on an upcoming project. It includes a letter stating "our management team feels that customer service is of utmost importance" and a five-page credit application which asks, among other things, for my personal net worth, the type of car I drive and the names of my children.

I write down $13.52, a 1952 Studebaker, and Jesus, Mary and Joseph and fax it back.

An hour later I receive a call. My application is approved.

1 p.m.: A client calls. A month ago I spent two hours on a call with this same client, who requested a massive load of work overnight. I did the work and got it to him. I heard nothing. Turns out he went on vacation.

Today he phones to arrange a conference call at which his co-workers will be present to discuss the project.

He says, "I gave you a bunch of objectives and strategies. But I don't remember them. Can you review your notes and e-mail my objectives and strategies before the call, so I'll look like I know what I'm talking about?"

He then tells me he has just been promoted.

4 p.m.: Another call, this time from the service manager at the dealership where I had taken my car two weeks ago for a repair I was assured should take no more than three hours. A week later, after I called twice each day to request a status update, usually having to leave voicemail messages that weren't returned, I was notified the car was ready.

Three days later I received a call from the manufacturer, asking me to rate my satisfaction with the dealer's service department. I reported I was not pleased.

This afternoon the service manager calls, berating me for being honest, and promising worse service in the future as payback.

7 p.m.: I arrive home to find the security alarm screeching as a result of a power surge, sending our traumatized dachshunds under our bed from which they won't emerge. Unable to find the key to the control box, I finally rip the wires from the wall, and take my family to a Mexican restaurant.

We are surrounded by toddlers shrieking at the top of their lungs while their parents look on approvingly, and by mariachis singing "Guantanamera" who won't go away until I slip them a five dollar bill.

I most definitely need a vacation.

Perhaps a nice inn in Vermont, where I can leave this crazy world behind.

Your airline of choice

I've never forgotten my first flight. It was from St. Louis to Washington, D.C. I was 11.

Even though jets had been introduced years before, Eastern Airlines was still flying four-engine Electra props between the two cities.

En route we touched down at Evansville and Louisville, cities that seemed impossibly exotic and sophisticated to a boy from Auxvasse, Mo.

I remember the hot meal served on real china, the pretty stewardess who brought pillows and blankets (as if I could sleep when there was so much to see) and how my mother insisted that I wear a coat and tie because, she said, everyone on the plane would be dressed up. (They were.)

That first round-trip flight was so wonderful that I would have remained loyal to Eastern Airlines for life had its management and unions not forgotten that it existed first and foremost to treat its customers well.

Deservedly so, Eastern was one of the first major airlines to go belly-up. Other airlines that, like Eastern, dominated the skies when I was a boy (e.g. Pan Am, TWA,) have also ceased to exist… and at least one more of the majors is also headed toward oblivion.

I enjoy opening my *Wall Street Journal* and finding stories about the financial woes afflicting the major airlines. Having treated customers like lepers for years, they deserve everything that's happening to them.

Have you tried to complain to an airline lately? I did after one recent flight and learned that, thanks to e-mail, airlines don't even have to station human beings in their complaint departments. They can simply program their computers to return one of dozens of canned responses.

To: Customer Service @ ConglomAir.com
Sent: March 31, 4:40 PM
From: Thomas Dryden
Re: Abysmal service

I was a passenger on Flight 666 to Chicago yesterday. The flight was delayed due to mechanical problems when the control tower noticed as we were taxiing that the left wing of the aircraft was missing. The pilot returned to the terminal to discharge passengers, who were told to wait in the gate area until a replacement plane arrived. I'm not complaining about that—nobody wants to fly an unsafe plane. I am writing to express my displeasure with the manner in which

To: Thomas Dryden
Sent: March 31, 4:41 PM
From: Customer Service @ ConglomAir.com
Re: File No. 5256-88-44306-A

Please note that, due to the high volume of mail we receive, incoming emails are limited to 400 characters. We consider feedback from our passengers to be very important. We are currently experiencing higher than normal email communications and our response to you may be delayed. Thank you for your patience.

> To: Customer Service @ ConglomAir.com
> Sent: March 31, 4:45 PM
> From: Thomas Dryden
> Re: I WASN'T FINISHED!

During the 11 hours we waited for a replacement aircraft, your ground crew made a grand total of four announcements regarding the status of Flight 666, leaving passengers wondering if and when we would get to Chicago. I overheard a lady in a wheelchair who was worried about missing her connecting flight to Tokyo ask how far she would have to travel to get to her gate at O'Hare. The agent told her, "How would I know? I've never been to Michigan." Chicago isn't even in Michi

> To: Thomas Dryden
> Sent: March 31, 4:46 PM
> From: Customer Service @ ConglomAir.com
> Re: File No. 5873-13-94733-R

Weather, air traffic, mechanical difficulties and other circumstances beyond our control sometimes cause delayed or canceled flights. Although no airline can guarantee flight schedules, ConglomAir emphasizes the highest level of customer service. Please accept our sincere apologies for any inconvenience.

> To: Customer Service @ ConglomAir.com
> Sent: March 31, 4:51 PM
> From: Thomas Dryden
> Re: Flight from hell

By the time the replacement plane arrived at midnight, the crew had been on duty 14 hours and was unable to fly. The back-up crew was en route from Miami. When they landed at 3 a.m. and we finally boarded, the lead flight attendant got on the P.A. and announced she didn't want to be there any more than we did. She said she had been on her feet all day, was hungry, missed her husband, and was sick of management treating her like pond scu

To: Thomas Dryden
Sent: March 31, 4:52 PM.
From: Customer Service @ ConglomAir.com
Re: File No. 6113-42-2654-X

TPS (Total Passenger Satisfaction) is our primary goal. We will get back to you as soon as we have investigated your complaint.

To: Customer Service @ ConglomAir.com
Sent: March 31, 4:55 PM
From: Thomas Dryden
Re: Flight from hell

When I found my seat, I immediately noticed a foul odor coming from the seat pocket in front of me. It contained a dead cat, whose tail came off in my hand. The man across the aisle was a pathologist. He said it was clear to him that the cat had been decomposing for several weeks, perhaps as long as a month. I know there isn't always time for a thorough cabin cleaning between flights and recognize that ConglomAir is in dire financial straits, but can't help wondering if

To: Thomas Dryden
Sent: March 31, 4:56 PM.
From: Customer Service @ ConglomAir.com

AT 50, YOUR WARRANTY EXPIRES

Re: File No. 7019-58-5638-C

Your constructive comment(s) has/have been noted and we thank you for taking the time to contact us. We look forward to continue being your airline of choice.

It's that least wonderful time

My least favorite day each year is the day of my annual colonoscopy during which a doctor inserts what appears to be a steel garden hose with a video camera up a passage I don't want to identify in case you're reading this while eating Fritos with refried bean dip or some other favorite comfort food.

My second least-favorite day is the day each year I meet with my CPA during which I turn over records that will enable him and his cipher-nerds to prepare my tax returns.

When completed on April 15th at noon, each return will be approximately as thick as *The Brothers Karamazov* (and I'm talking Dostoevsky's handwritten manuscript, not the paperback).

I sign them without understanding a single entry.

Taxes are gobbledygook to me. Like many writers, I was born without the brain lobe that processes numbers. I only went as far as subtraction in high school general math class, for which I earned a gentleman's "D" (but only because the teacher was a family friend).

Every year, I borrow my wife's station wagon to haul to my accountant credit card receipts, canceled checks, unopened envelopes from banks and brokerage firms,

1099s, 747-400s, and, of course, a color Polaroid of the inside of my colon to prove I underwent a delicate medical procedure and should therefore be entitled to deduct it.

Like everything I think I should be able to deduct, he always tells me I can't.

I don't get deductions. Literally or figuratively. For example, I pay massive amounts each year to provide health, dental and life insurance for my company's employees and their families. They don't report the amount I pay on their behalf as income, it's an "employee benefit."

But my family's share of that is treated as income, and I have to pay taxes on it.

Then I get to deduct part of it. At least I think I do.

So confusing.

But it used to be simple.

Early in my career, when most of my income went to car payments, I would go to H&R Block, show my W-2, pay $20, and get back a two-page return.

I always received a refund.

In my late twenties, my income went up when I started working for a Manhattan ad agency.

Someone's Uncle Sid specialized in accounting for creative types so, like my co-workers, I went to him to have my taxes done.

"So how much did you pay for those orthopedic shoes?" Sid asked two seconds after we met.

"They're not orthopedic, they're Cole-Haans." I answered.

"Well, they're orthopedic now, so you have every right to deduct them," said Sid, producing a handful of receipts from a Brighton Beach orthopedic shoe store. "Your wife wears orthopedic shoes, too."

Sid was clearly a creative type too, so we hit it off from the get-go.

You name it, Sid wrote it off.

Cable TV bills? Deductible.

"You're in advertising, you need to watch commercials."

A veterinary bill for removing the dog's kidney stones? Deductible.

"You took her to casting calls for Chuck Wagon commercials, didn't you?"

A Greek vacation?

"No problem, you were location scouting."

Needless to say, when Sid did my taxes, I always got a huge refund, which was, of course, deductible on the next year's return.

That ended the year Sid relocated to Kansas—a town called Leavenworth, I believe—and I started my own ad agency.

I switched to a bona fide CPA who understood terms like the "GDS and ADS assets placed in service in tax years beginning before 2000" he had to account for on last year's returns.

I'm not complaining about paying taxes, I understand why they are needed. But why must they be so bloody complicated?

What is a ratably allocated itemized deduction?

A long-term capital loss carryover?

The alternative minimum foreign tax credit?

Beats me, but the CPA says I apparently suffer from all these afflictions.

But maybe they're desirable. Who knows?

All I know for sure is that I haven't received a refund since my salad days with Sid. Whether I've had a good year or bad, I always have to pay far more than I've already paid in.

My point, in case you're wondering, is this: When you get down to it, taxes and colonoscopies are a lot alike.

I'll let you finish that thought, and get back to your bean dip.

Enjoy it.

Daniel Boone would disown me

I am a great-great-great nephew of Daniel Boone, the legendary pioneer who single-handedly hacked his way from the Carolinas across the Cumberland Gap to Kentucky and on to Missouri, encountering along the way savage Indians, ferocious bears and—worst of all—not a single Ritz-Carlton. Not even a Holiday Inn.

Now Daniel Boone was a man—yes, a big man—with an eye like an eagle, tall as a mountain, brave, fearless and tough as a mighty oak tree.

Unfortunately, I am no Daniel Boone.

At my advanced age, I can't handle the climate, pestilence and wild animals of suburban Connecticut, much less Indians, bears or lack of turndown service.

As I write this, I'm trying to avoid clearing the frog in my throat because doing so causes excruciating pain to my left side where I cracked a rib.

I was inching my way down my ski slope-steep driveway the morning after a snow/rain storm to fetch my *USA Today*. The pavement was a sheet of ice.

Halfway down the hill, I slipped and—ka-boom—landed flat on my back.

My wife, who was watching from kitchen, ran to the door. "You OK?"

"Yes," I answered weakly, struggling to regain my breath which had been knocked from me along with my pride.

That afternoon the rib began to throb. That night, the pain was so intense I couldn't sleep. The next morning I went to the walk-in clinic for X-rays. The doctor prescribed painkillers, which helped, but not much.

A cracked rib only adds to my misery because I'm feeling lousy from my most recent bout with Lyme disease for which I'm on a second round of antibiotics.

Lyme disease is another hazard of living in Connecticut, where it's normal to see people walking around town hooked up to IV drips.

Then there are the wild animals of Connecticut, including, of course, the deer that carry Lyme spirochete-infected ticks.

As I was barreling down the Merritt Parkway several years ago, one charged at my car. Both the car (it was two weeks old) and deer were totaled.

Last year my teenage son was driving his Honda Civic home from school in a line of traffic moving 20 mph on a nearby street. A friend and our younger son were with him.

A deer bounded out of the woods and into their path…realized it was going to be hit…and attempted to leap over the Honda. It smashed through the windshield and came to rest on the console.

But for the grace of God and the inventor of the safety-glass windshield (which shattered into a million shards, wrapping itself around the boys' faces), nobody was injured (except the deer, which had to be shot).

My wife swooned when she saw the car's blood-drenched interior.

Daniel fought bears. I live in terror of coyotes. A pack of 'em killed our beagle, Bella, two years ago in our yard.

Yesterday was the last straw.

I went outside with Bonnie, our dachshund. She immediately ran around the side of the house from which I heard a terrible commotion—barking, snarling, yelping.

She was face-to-face with a giant raccoon which shouldn't have been out and about at 2 p.m. because coons are nocturnal unless, of course, they have rabies.

I swooped her up and ran inside.

I'm almost sure Bonnie didn't come into direct contact with the coon. If she did, she's safe—she's had rabies shots.

But always the hypochondriac—most of Daniel's descendants are—I'm now worried that some of the coon's saliva may have gotten on me, which means I'll get rabies.

I looked up the symptoms and learned that if I start talking gibberish, it's a sign I have it.

I don't think that I can take it.

'Cause it took so long to bake it.

And I'll never have that recipe again.

Oh no.

Charlton Heston drops in

I almost hired a Harvard MBA to work for my ad agency once.
It was the third interview that did him in. I sprang my favorite interview question, "What's your favorite TV show?"
"I never watch TV," he sniffed.
I showed him the door.
I believe that if you're going to be in a business that targets the masses, you have to be a member of the masses yourself. You need to read the *Post*, eat at McDonald's and, especially, watch the tube.
Unfortunately, I wouldn't be able to hire myself these days.
Cablevision delivers 108 channels. There's nothing on any of them I watch regularly. I no longer care about mind-numbingly predictable comedies, the look-alike news magazines, whodunit murder mysteries or which bachelor/ette is about to be told to take a hike.
Most nights, I read books.
I only watch TV if there's a laughably bad old movie playing, like the one American Movie Classics ran the other night, the dumbest movie ever made—*Airport '75*.
Here's the plot.

Karen Black is a stewardess (that's "flight attendant" for my PC readers).

Her lover, Charlton Heston, is chief pilot for the airline.

The movie begins as passengers board a 747 to LA piloted by Efrem Zimbalist, Jr., assisted by co-pilot Roy Thinnes, and navigator Erik Estrada.

Black is the lead stew, capably assisted in the rear cabin by a buxom blonde, Christopher Norris from *Trapper John M.D.* (Did you ever wonder why her parents named her Christopher? Me, too. Not that I obsessed about it or anything, but I definitely thought about it every time I saw her on the tube.)

Passengers include a nun (Helen Reddy); a teenage dialysis patient on a stretcher (Linda Blair, fresh from her head-turning, Campbell's Split Pea Soup-hurling role as a possessed child in *The Exorcist*); a hack actor (Sid Caesar); a little old lady who swills boilermakers (Myrna Loy); inebriated businessmen (Norman Fell and Jerry Stiller), and Gloria Swanson as herself.

Waiting at LAX are Heston (who's planning a heart-to-heart talk with Black, hopefully about how she needs surgery to uncross her eyes if she wants to keep her job because her condition is distracting) and the airline's chief mechanic (George Kennedy) whose wife (Susan Clark) and bratty kid are on the soon-to-be ill-fated jet.

After take-off, Black and Norris go to the cockpit to serve coffee, tea or whatever.

The pilots, as pilots did back in those days when flying was fun, sexually harass them, but they take it in stride. (Today, they would whip out their cell phones and call ahead to have the pigs arrested when the plane landed, then they would sue the airline.)

Back in the orange, yellow and purple-accented cabin, Reddy seeks out the sick child (Blair) and sings her a reassuring song (not "I Am Woman"—nuns back then didn't buy off on that stuff) while strumming a guitar.

I would have enlisted fellow passengers to pin her to the floor and duct-tape her mouth shut.

Meanwhile, somewhere out west, businessman Dana Andrews is taking off in his single engine Cessna 172.

As the passenger jet nears Salt Lake City, Andrews suffers a heart attack and his plane, which has magically morphed into a twin-engine Baron, crashes head-on into the 747, shattering its windshield and leaving a gaping hole in the fuselage.

Thinnes is sucked out into thinnes air, Zimbalist is blinded, Estrada is killed.

Ditzy Black doesn't get on the intercom and ask if there's a pilot in the house. That would have been too logical.

Instead, she takes over the controls while the other stewardesses serve cocktails to the amazingly calm passengers, who are probably blotto from the complimentary drinks not to mention oxygen-deprivation.

With Heston providing encouragement by radio as he races toward Salt Lake in a Lear, Black pilots the stricken 747 through canyons and over mountaintops, which the jumbo jet clears by inches.

Realizing his beloved can't land the 747, Heston is dropped into the cockpit from a jet helicopter.

Though there's no windshield, his toupee remains firmly cemented to his head, and, as they touch down safely, Black snuggles up against him looking dreamy-eyed. (I think—who can tell?)

The cabin crew efficiently evacuates passengers down emergency slides. In a bus taking them to the terminal, Swanson tells a youthful passenger who has commented on the glorious day, "Every morning is beautiful. You're just too young to know it."

If CBS, NBC or ABC would greenlight a series as hilarious as *Airport '75* wasn't supposed to be, I'd watch it every night of the week.

'Till they do (or until *Airport '77*, scheduled to air next month), it's back to the books for me.

New Jersey's next Poet Laureate

Last week the New Jersey Senate voted to eliminate the position of State Poet Laureate after the current title holder, Amiri Baraka, wrote a poem implying that Israel knew about the World Trade Center attack in advance.

Three words of advice for those legislators: Not so fast. Go ahead, fire Baraka, he's a dope. But don't eliminate the job.

I want it.

After all, I come from a long line of Poet Laureates.

Back in 1668, a guy named John Dryden was named Poet Laureate of England, a fact that earned me brownie points from every English professor I ever had in college.

Like my esteemed ancestor, I believe that poetry plays a pivotal role as a civilizing force in society.

OK, I don't live in New Jersey. So what? You don't have to live in a state to capture its essence in verse, as you'll see in these sample poems reflecting a wide range of styles I'm going to submit in the hopes the legislators will change their minds.

Ode to Atlantic City
Strolling the boardwalk, holding hands
Past Bally's, Caesar's and the Sands.
Buying cheesy souvenirs,
Swilling sweaty ice-cold beers.

Bathers frolic in the surf
Outside a hotel owned by Merv.
A tourist on a gambling tryst,
Asks her lover, "What ocean's this?"

Atlantic City, how I love thee,
Oh town that birthed Monopoly!
You once were known as just a dump,
But that was before Donald Trump.

Burt Parks is surely smiling down
From heaven, on his favorite town.
So when I die, please bury me
Beneath thy boardwalk, by the sea.

Coming Home
Standing in the IKEA parking lot opposite
Newark Liberty Airport,
watching planes touch down
from all over the world,
drawn to Jersey like a baby to its mother's breast—
Continental, United and Northwest,
from Akron, Bangkok and Trieste,
bringing home native sons and daughters
who cannot wait to disembark
and inhale deeply the Jersey air they cannot

expunge from their lungs no matter where they roam.
The EPA may say it stinks
but to them it smells of home.

Demographics
Newjerseyisthemostdenselypopulatedstateintheunion.
Which means there is more love per square mile
in Jersey than anyplace in America.

**Stopping at the Joyce Kilmer Rest Area
on the Jersey Turnpike**
I think that I shall never see
Such a Lysol-clean facility,
Named after him who did write "Trees."
Oops, I must've left my keys

At Roy Rogers, where I did feast
On the best fried chicken in the east.
And then to Starbucks I did go,
For a cup of steamy Joe

To stay awake on this long ride
Through the Jersey countryside.
Past factories, farms, fields, malls and hills
And the home of Carter's Liver Pills.

Poems are written by fools like me,
The next Laureate of New Jersey.

    Whattya think? Should I apply for the job or not?

Harassment 101

Dear Employee:

We hope you found Megacorp's Sexual Harassment Seminar to be a productive and positive learning experience.

Now it's time to apply what you have learned over the last five days to your everyday job. Please complete the following quiz which will be placed in your personnel file so that, in the event you are ever charged with sexual harassment, Megacorp will be able to assist in your defense by proving that we tried to train you.

Remember our number one goal for next year: Harassment-free in 2003!

A co-worker comes to work wearing a low-cut see-through blouse with a black lace Miracle bra underneath it, a micro-mini skirt, and make-up that makes Mimi of the *Drew Carey Show* look like Mother Teresa. What do you do?

    a. Take up a collection for a Talbot's gift certificate and present it in a birthday card, even though it is not the employee's birthday

    b. Call Human Resources

    c. Wear sunglasses, explaining you just came from the opthamologist, so you cannot be accused of leering
    d. Inform him that his outfit is inappropriate

    At an office holiday party, a male co-worker tells you "you look nice tonight." You should:
    a. Call the police
    b. Notify Human Resources first thing Monday
    c. Throw a glass of punch in his face
    d. Ask if the name Lorena Bobbitt rings a bell

    During your annual performance review in her office, your boss suddenly announces "it's hot in here" and removes her blouse. You:
    a. Agree with her, and volunteer to open the window a crack
    b. Call Human Resources
    c. Steer the conversation back to your on-the-job performance
    d. Offer to get her a drink of water

    At the copy machine, a co-worker is telling a "joke" about a priest, a rabbi, an Islamic cleric and a farmer's daughter. What should you do?
    a. Drown out the punchline by pretending to have a coughing fit
    b. Ask the co-worker to e-mail the so-called "joke" so you can send it to friends. Forward it instead to Human Resources for follow-up
    c. Remind the co-worker that ethnic jokes hurt innocent people. Say something like, "As a Catholic married to a Jew raising our children in the Islamic faith while living on a farm, you are making me uncomfortable"

d. Imagine your dog was just run over to prevent you from inadvertently smiling, even though you are deeply offended

A co-worker confides that his or her boss brushed against him or her in a crowded elevator. What's your best choice?
   a. Buy your co-worker a can of mace
   b. Determine if you work in a one-story building. If you do, this despicable incident may have occurred in a hotel in which case you should call the boss's spouse to arrange transportation to the nearest mental health clinic
   c. Call Human Resources
   d. Immediately take the co-worker to the hospital for a pelvic exam

While traveling on business in a distant city with a co-worker of the opposite sex, you are snowed in. There is only one available hotel room in the entire town. You:
   a. Each rent cars and drive back to the home office through the blizzard
   b. Both sleep on the floor at the airport, in separate concourses
   c. Agree to share the room, but purchase a gun (you may put it on your expense account) in case s/he makes offensive suggestions
   d. Call Human Resources

I brake for bumper stickers

You don't see many bumper stickers here in Fairfield County, Conn.

Stickers always leave a gooey residue that's hard to remove and when you're driving a leased luxury vehicle as so many Fairfield Countians do, you don't want to have to pay a fee to restore it to its original condition at the end of the lease term.

If it's bumper stickers you want, you need to head to college towns where you'll see stickers announcing students' idealistic views, to the Bible Belt where the faithful proclaim their love of love of Jesus on their minivans, or to places like Vermont where old hippies go to live out their Geritol years.

I've never met a bumper sticker I didn't like, even if I didn't agree with the message.

I admire folks who have the courage to festoon their vehicles with their own personal opinions.

People who put bumper stickers on their cars aren't afraid to speak out—something all too rare in today's P.C. society where everyone is afraid of offending everyone else.

The other day I was following an SUV driven by a blonde. The back window displayed a decal announcing she had gone to an elite liberal arts college. Affixed to the bumper was a sticker that said, "Abolish Land Mines."

While that driver may have had the grades, SAT scores and/or connections to get into a swell college, she's three pickles short of a barrel.

If she wants to influence people who are actually in a position to abolish land mines, she shouldn't be driving through suburban Connecticut.

She should be driving through Chechnya, Afghanistan or Angola where the people who bury land mines live.

Maybe land mine-buriers would see her sticker and decide to dig them up. But I somehow doubt it.

She's as naïve about how the world works as people who display "Envision World Peace" stickers (they should be driving through Fallujah or along the DMZ between North and South Korea) and "Free Tibet" stickers (who should be driving past Tiananmen Square).

This being an election year, there's a plethora of bumper stickers announcing drivers' choices for president.

Driving the 120 miles from Raleigh to Wilmington through John Edwards' home state of North Carolina recently, I counted four Kerry/Edwards and 11 Bush/Cheney 2004 stickers, one of which was affixed to a Mercedes 500. (Note: If you drive an expensive car, a Bush/Cheney sticker may remind the driver of the 1987 Toyota Celica following you down the highway that, thanks to Bush, you got a tax break, making it possible for you to upgrade to a Mercedes 500 from a 230. Your bumper sticker might actually work to your candidate's disadvantage.)

While there may not be as many pro-Kerry stickers as pro-Bush—I don't know anyone who is passionately for Kerry, only folks who are against Bush—there are lots of anti-Bush stickers out there, like "When Clinton Lied, Nobody Died" (slapping two presidents upside the head for the price of one bumper sticker), "Re-defeat Bush," and a sticker I saw affixed to a beat-up Saab parked on the street in Soho, featuring the silhouetted heads of Bush, Cheney, Ashcroft and Rumsfeld: "Don't Change Horsemen in the Middle of an Apocalypse."

Religious bumper stickers abound: "My boss is a Jewish Carpenter"..."America Needs a Faith Lift"... and—my favorite—"Non-Exposure To The Son Will Cause Burning."

Infidels counter with bumper stickers such as "You Make Jesus Vomit" and "Don't Pray In My Schools and I Won't Think In Your Church."

The best bumper stickers, however, reveal nothing about the driver's politics or religion. Their only communications objective is to make you laugh. Examples:

"Envision Whirled Peas."

"Free Tibet. (With the purchase of a 44 oz. drink.)"

"So Many Cats, So Few Recipes."

"If You Can Read This, I've Lost My Trailer."

"I Still Miss My Ex But My Aim Is Improving."

"I'm Dating Your Husband."

The funniest bumper sticker I've seen lately—one that made me laugh out loud—was on a Ford pick-up with West Virginia plates in a Raleigh parking garage: "My Kid Sells Term Papers to Your Honor Student."

I have a feeling the driver of that truck and I would get along just fine.

How to succeed in business

The other day I saw a businessman who was reading a book entitled "Implementing Your Strategic Plan: How to Turn Intent into Effective Action for Sustainable Change."

He was highlighting entire paragraphs with a yellow marker.

I had to restrain myself from grabbing the book, smacking him over the head with it, and telling him that if he wants to put his plans into action, he shouldn't be reading, he should be *doing something*.

I can't believe the plethora of business books on the market—books with titles like "Why Decisions Fail" (because they were idiotic in the first place) and Jack and Suzy Welch's "Winning" (hire good people, empower them, then fire ten percent of them every year to keep those that are left behind scared witless).

Problem is, almost all these business advice books are written for management types. What the world really needs is a practical business book for worker-bees—the people who actually get things done in today's top-heavy organizations. So I'm writing one, following a Q and A format.

Here are excerpts.

Q: A business associate has his assistant place his phone calls for him. It drives me nuts to pick up the phone and hear her say, "Please hold for Mr. Smythe." It's as if he is announcing his time is more valuable than mine. What can I do?

A: Take the call and say "Hi Ralph" (whatever his name is, call him Ralph—he's already insecure which is why he feels the need to appear important, so reinforce that insecurity by acting like you don't know who he is). "My phone number is 203-555-1234. Program it into your speed-dial and call me yourself from now on because I've got better things to do than wait for you to get on the line. In fact, why not try it now to make sure it works?" Then hang up.

Q: I am ill at ease and have nothing to contribute when co-workers gossip around the water cooler. Suggestions?

A: You'll enjoy office gossip much more when you feel like a contributor, so here's a conversation starter: "Do you believe that story about the actor and the hamster?"

Q: I've been a stay-at-home mom for 15 years but will soon be going back to work for a company that encourages "business casual" attire. I have no idea what that means. What should I wear my first day?

A: Have you regained the firm, flat tummy you had B.C. (before children)? If so, a spandex midriff-baring tank top is perfect. If not, go for one that covers it.

Q: I'm a divisional sales manager of my company and become extremely nervous before quarterly meetings in which I must present my division's results to my regional VP. I sweat uncontrollably, stammer and once had to sit down to keep from swooning. What can I do?

A: Vodka. (I like Gray Goose.) It's odorless and clear so you can fill a water bottle and take swigs before and during your presentation. If your boss is so clueless he needs a meeting to find out how your division is doing, he won't notice—trust me on this.

Remember not to put olives in the bottle!

Q: My do-nothing supervisor takes credit for my work. The latest: Last week I emailed her a courtesy copy of a presentation I had been working on for weeks, showing how the company could save $1 million annually. Expressing "concerns," she ordered me not to send it to the company president. She then forwarded it to the president with a note claiming the ideas were hers. I was furious. What should I do?

A: Tomorrow stick your head in her office, say you're going for coffee and offer to get her a cup. Then put Ex-Lax in it.

Q: A co-worker uses extremely course language. How can I let him know he is making me uncomfortable?

A: Tell the SOB to shut the f--- up or you'll report his miserable a-- to Human Resources. Then change the subject. For example, "What do you think about those Mets?"

Q: My co-workers spend the day cruising the Internet and placing personal phone calls. I think this is tantamount to stealing. What can I do to encourage them to use the company's time more productively?

A: I notice you sent this question on company letterhead and ran the letter through the company's postage meter. Sanctimonious hypocrites like you make me want to puke.

Have questions you want answered? Send them my way!

Seems like a fair trade to me

An Oklahoma woman was arrested recently when she attempted to trade her newborn baby for a Chihuahua.

As the father of two human and two canine children, I don't understand why the police and media are treating her like a nut case. Human kids are high maintenance. Dogs—especially small breeds like Chihuahuas—aren't.

Consider the following.

Within a week after you bring him home from the kennel, your Chihuahua sleeps through the night. As the parent of a human child, you won't experience an uninterrupted night's sleep for the next 20 years.

A human child doesn't have the ability to hike his leg on your brand-new upholstered sofa. A Chihuahua, on the other hand, never spills Mountain Dew into the soundboard of your baby grand.

On road trips, you don't have to play Barney CDs for hours on end to keep your Chihuahua quiet until, in desperation, you seriously consider crashing the car into an overpass to make the noise stop.

You don't have to buy an SUV to haul your Chihuahua and his or her sports equipment around town. (Of course, you don't have to buy one for your human child either unless he or she is the size of Refrigerator Perry, in which case you should be spending your money on an endocrinologist instead of on a vehicle that gets 10 miles per gallon.)

From the time your human child is five until he or she is old enough to drive, you'll devote your Saturdays to shuttling the kid from game to game. Chihuahuas don't play soccer, football, hockey, baseball, t-ball, lacrosse or basketball. As a Chihuahua parent, you can enjoy an additional 626 days –1.7 years—of free time.

Chihuahuas don't tie up your phone for hours, yakking with friends.

At your home computer, you're never interrupted by pop-up Instant Messages from your Chihuahua's teenage amigos who have screen names like Papa Zit.

Chihuahuas don't hog your big-screen TV watching ESPN, MTV or *South Park*. And they don't get into barking matches with one another over who controls the remote.

You'll never have to sit in the passenger seat of your car, frozen with terror, as your 16-year-old Chihuahua, learner's permit in paw, navigates curvy rain-slicked roads dodging stone fences, mailboxes and oncoming cars being driven at 60 mph by 17-year-old Chihuahuas listening to Eminem CDs.

You'll never have to wait up until 2 a.m., worried your Chihuahua is out doing God knows what with God knows whom. When you hear a siren wailing, you won't automatically assume it's headed to either arrest your Chihuahua or to scrape what's left of him off the road. He is curled up at the foot of your bed, snoring peacefully.

You won't have to work 10 years past the time you

could have otherwise retired to send your Chihuahua to college. An eight-week basic obedience class costs $100.

And if your Chihuahua decides to go for a graduate degree, an intermediate class is another $100.

You'll never have to walk your female Chihuahua down the aisle and give her in marriage to some mongrel she met in a bar you've told her 50 times is going to make her life a living hell but she won't listen.

If your Chihuahua gets the urge to mate, simply place her in a room with a male Chihuahua and—voila—nine weeks later, adorable offspring who won't call you Grandma or Grandpa. (Of course, this will never happen because you will have your Chihuahua neutered. That's something you can't do with children either.)

Chihuahuas don't leave wet towels on hardwood floors.

You'll never feel shamed into taking your Chihuahua to Disney World, because every other Chihuahua in town has been there except yours.

You'll never get a terse call from your Chihuahua's teacher demanding a face-to-face conference.

On the other hand, Chihuahuas don't make homemade Father's Day cards you save in your sock drawer, precious mementos that would be the first thing you would grab if the house caught fire.

They never win academic awards, or varsity letters.

They never make you proud by portraying Prospero in fourth grade productions of "The Tempest."

And they can't play "Moonlight Sonata" flawlessly at piano recitals.

I'm convinced they would if they could, but their little paws simply aren't big enough.

While you were sleeping

One of the many bizarre afflictions of middle age is having to get up every morning precisely at 3:05 a.m. to pee.

Once I relieve my bladder (which takes twice as long as it used to thanks to my prostate, a gland I've read will almost certainly turn cancerous if I live long enough), I'm wide awake.

So I wander into the family room, plop down on the sofa and turn on the TV, looking desperately for something boring (e.g. C-Span) or inane (e.g. a *Petticoat Junction* re-run) to lull me back to sleep.

Instead, I find 106 channels playing informercials.

"...the versatile new appliance all America is talking about, the Scuz-a-Way Steamer. Yours for just three easy payments of $19.95. Call right now and we'll even include..." (Channel Up)

"... YES, Jesus wants you to be RICH...to live in a nice house or late-model mobile home...to drive a fancy car or pickup...to have a big-screen TV...to live a life of ABUNDANCE, but if, and only if..." (Channel Up)

"...not only rids your body of toxins but, in seven short days, Nature's Natural Cleanser leaves you up to 20 pounds lighter, literally flushing fat from your system just like nature intended..." (Channel Up)

"...where it's lightly raining. Moving to the west, it's a chilly 11 degrees in Missoula, a comfy 67 in Phoenix and LA reports 64 with dense smog and occasional light-to-moderate fires in the Hollywood Hills. Up in Seattle, we have..." (Channel Up)

"...all with no money down, Bob. Today we're the proud owners of a six-unit apartment building, two duplexes and three single-family houses that together pay us income of $1,200 a month. I ain't never gonna work again and neither's Earlene. Heck, the day we got our first rent check, she told her boss down at the shoe factory to take her job and shove it ..." (Channel Up)

"...such awful panic that my stomach would start churning and I'd get diarrhea whenever I had to meet anyone new. Needless to say, I'd pretty much given up on dating much less ever finding a husband until a friend told me about the Great Plains Center for Anxiety Management and its founder, Dr. Lucretia Beagle, whose relaxation tapes, I'm here to tell you, saved my..." (Channel Up)

"... combination microwave/deep fat fryer/bread machine/ salad spinner/rotisserie oven that, in minutes, enables you to prepare nutritious meals your whole family will love. And best of all, you just set it and forget it while..." (Channel Up)

AT 50, YOUR WARRANTY EXPIRES

"...in seconds, using ordinary tap water, the amazing Scuz-a-Way steam-cleans precious jewelry like this ...baked-on oven grease like this, just wipe it away ...your car's engine...steams wallpaper off plaster walls ...steam-cleans odors out of even the stinkiest sneakers, leaving them smelling and looking brand new...even steams the wrinkles out of delicate silks, saving you thousands of..." (Channel Up)

"...toll-free number and say, 'Billy Bob, I don't have an extra $50 to tithe to the Tabernacle this very minute.' And you know what our operators are gonna tell you? They're gonna say, 'That's OK, Jesus LOVES you and so does Brother Billy Bob. We know you wanna give as much as you can and that you wanna give it now, not a week from now. That's why we take Visa, Mastercard, and Discover...'" (Channel Up)

"...passed a 20-foot long tapeworm she didn't even know she had. And that's not all she lost. Her very first month, 47 pounds of fat melted away with no exercise whatsoever. All she took was five of these tiny Nature's Natural Cleanser pills every morning with a glass of water. Just look at these before and after..." (Channel Up)

"...and in Connecticut's Fairfield County, up to six feet are expected by noon north of the Merritt Parkway..." (Channel Up)

"...we go from door to door the first day of ever month and pocket the cash or money orders our tenants fork over, then me and Earlene git in the car and laugh all the way to the bank because it didn't cost us nothing thanks to…" (Channel Up)

"…so nervous I'd throw up whenever my boss walked into my cubicle. Then I saw Dr. Beagle on *Good Morning Scranton*. She was talking about something she called a panic attack and a bell went off inside my head …" (Channel Up)

…beautiful rack of lamb (APPLAUSE)…golden brown fries (APPLAUSE)…a loaf of crusty, piping-hot bread (APPLAUSE)… crisp garden salad (APPLAUSE) and, for dessert, this mouth-watering apple brown betty (APPLAUSE)…all from the same appliance, and all ready in less than 15 minutes …" (Power Off)

'Till we meet again.
And again. And again.

I left corporate America and struck out on my own when I was still in my twenties. I had to. I was accomplishing nothing.

Why? Because, like everyone else in the ad agency where I was employed at the time, I was spending 99 percent of every day attending meetings, in which we all sat around a conference room table attempting to reach something called "consensus."

Consensus, if you ask me, is senseless.

So are meetings.

When I started my own agency, I made sure there was no conference room. Fifteen years later, there still isn't.

Unfortunately, our clients do have conference rooms and they use them. At one company, rooms need to be booked six months in advance. And it's not like they're scarce. There are four per floor.

Have you ever tried to reach someone in corporate America? Forget it. They're in meetings. I'll call a client and hear a taped message. "Hi, this is Edgar, I'm in an all-day meeting but I'll be checking my voicemail during breaks, so if leave your number I'll get right back to you. If you need to speak to someone immediately, please dial zero for my assistant, Eunice."

So I'll dial zero. "Hi, this is Eunice. I'm in a training meeting but if you'll leave your name and number..."

I once called a client who—duh—was in a meeting. When she called back, she reported without a trace of irony that her boss had called a meeting about how to run more efficient meetings.

Since I can never reach clients on the phone and they can never get to their offices to retrieve e-mail, the only way to communicate is in person. Which means a face-to-face meeting.

I recently flew to Tampa for a meeting that was to begin at 9 a.m. When I arrived in the conference room, a Senior Vice President was taking breakfast orders, passing out menus from neighborhood delis.

After half an hour, the group reached consensus about which deli to order from. An hour later, a staffer returned with our collective order. No business was conducted during the meal, which lasted 30 minutes.

Once everyone had finished, a break was required so everyone could check voicemail. By the time the meeting got underway, it was 11:30 a.m.

When the projector was turned on, a bulb blew, so someone from the audiovisual department had to be called.

At noon, a staff member appeared with lunch menus. Following a lengthy discussion, the group failed to reach consensus, so it was decided that half would order Chinese, the rest would order Italian.

Three shopping bags of hot containers arrived at 1:45, the staffer went into the dining room, got plates and silverware, and set up a buffet atop a credenza. Then she took beverage orders.

An hour was spent eating, and another 15 minutes clearing the table during which more voicemail was checked.

By 3:45, just as a plate of pastries arrived, we were ready for business.

At that moment, the executive in charge of the meeting stood up, and announced he had to catch a flight to attend a meeting the next day in Seattle, as did five other attendees. They invited me to come along. I passed. I had to be in Charlotte. For a meeting, naturally. We agreed to reconvene in two weeks.

The day, however, wasn't a total loss. Everyone—even those of us who had ordered Chinese—was crazy about one of the dishes from the Italian restaurant, an extra rich variation of Fettucine Alfredo. It appeared the chef had simply made Alfredo sauce as usual, tossed it with al dente fettucine, plopped it in a casserole, topped the dish with mounds of parmesan and perhaps a bit of ricotta and broiled it until the cheese was crispy, chewy and brown.

As the one official act before the meeting was adjourned, it was decided the junior-most staff member would call the restaurant and ask for the recipe—the company is a big account so the restaurateur couldn't very well say no—and e-mail it to the rest of us.

Most productive meeting I've attended this millennium.

Saturday at the mall

Saturday morning, knowing my teenage son's '97 Civic needs a new battery, new tires and its first oil change of the millennium, I jumpstart it and take it to Sears Auto Center at the mall—a place I assiduously avoid since shopping, in my book, ranks just above a hemorrhoidectomy in terms of pleasurable activities.

Extracting a promise from the clerk to call my cell the moment the car is ready, I venture forth into a mall packed with stuff nobody needs but we Americans feel compelled to acquire in vast quantities because it's our birthright.

I start at the pet store, where puppies are displayed in tiered cages. All but one of the dogs, which include dachshunds, Cairns terriers, Chihuahuas, basset hounds and Pomeranians, are from the same breeder in Podunk, Kansas.

Our short-haired dachshund, Bonnie, is from a puppy mill in Arkansas. Swaybacked, bowlegged and territorial (she tried to bite my mother-in-law when she arrived for a visit), Bonnie's a prime example of why experts say you shouldn't buy dogs from pet stores though we, of course, worship the Oriental rugs she pees on. (Alas, poor Bonnie is also afflicted with an uncurable condition known as submissive urination).

Remembering our kitchen phone is dead, I stop by Radio Shack.

In the olden days, phones you rented from the phone company lasted a lifetime. Today you have to buy your own, need an electrical engineering degree to figure them out and most stop working after a couple of years.

I tell the clerk I want a cordless phone with a built-in answering machine.

"Digital or analog, 2.4 or 5.8 Gigahertz?" he asks.

"I dunno," I reply.

I buy one but have no idea what I bought.

Not having purchased anything new to wear for two years (other than a "Nixon in 2004" t-shirt which for some reason I found appealing), I wander into the men's department at Macy's.

Claiborne for Men features a brown polyester body shirt complete with spread collar. It looks like something John Travolta wore in *Saturday Night Fever*. Butt-ugly. Tommy Hilfiger, on the other hand, has a black shirt with tiny flowers. Very Carnaby Street. I wore one like it in college. It's tapered. So was I. Once.

The shirt evokes such fond memories I almost buy it until I remember I would look ridiculous.

Clothesless, I head for B. Dalton bookstore where I browse the biography section for half an hour. On my way out I notice a coffee table book entitled "Stay Tuned: TV's Most Unforgettable Moments" which includes a DVD of such memorable moments as Elvis' first appearance on *The Ed Sullivan Show* (I was four, my teenage sister screamed and wept, provoking my father to smack her upside the head), the rescue of little Jessica McClure (I read last week that she graduated from high school.

Well done, Jessie!) and the O.J. Bronco chase.

Originally $49.99, marked down to $6.99, I buy it. I'll get around to it some day. Probably in my retirement should I live so long.

Needing caffeine, I head for the food court. When my boys were little, we often took them to the mall on rainy Sunday afternoons. We'd give them money and let them pick out their own meals from the dozen or so junk-food restaurants, then they would ride the carousel at the far end of the food court.

Seems like yesterday, but our oldest just graduated from college. Our youngest is going 2,000 miles away to school in August.

I want to tell the parents sitting at tables ignoring their kids' animated chatter that it's the little moments— the Happy Meals in the food court at the mall—that someday they will yearn for most of all.

I return to Sears. The car still isn't ready. So I browse the Craftsman tools (my toolbox contains only a screwdriver and hammer), the plasma TVs (at $5,999 why not buy two? Wait—there's nothing on TV worth watching) and the Kenmore barbeque grills.

Having seen everything of possible interest in the mall, I cross the street to Puppy Love, another pet store. I'm playing with a beagle when my phone rings.

Good thing I have to leave. I was trying to figure out how to tell my wife that puppy had somehow found its way into my Radio Shack bag and I had no idea how it got there.

She wouldn't have been amused.

And Bonnie, our puppy mill princess, would have bitten him.

Many happy returns

Profound news for the unobservant: Men and women are different.

Example 1: A woman, upon entering a crowded supermarket parking lot with only a few open spaces around the perimeter, will never, ever park in one of those spaces. Instead, she'll sit in her car, waiting, until she sees a shopper emerging from the store. Then, like a lioness stalking a gazelle, she'll follow the shopper to his or her car...wait patiently, ignoring the seven cars and wailing ambulance lined up behind her, as the shopper loads the car with purchases and backs out...then park in the vacated space. She does this to be as close as possible to the entrance, failing to realize that, had she parked in one of the empty spots in the first place, she could have completed her shopping by now.

A man, when dispatched to the store for a loaf of bread, goes to a convenience store, leaves the motor running while he ducks in, and pays twice as much as he would have at the supermarket.

Example 2: Women love to shop.

Men would rather have gum surgery.

My own wife, for instance, says she considers shopping a form of relaxation.

I, on the other hand, shop only when necessary.

For instance, the time grease caught fire atop our stove, I went shopping for a fire extinguisher.

My wife informed me when I returned home and put out the flames that I had done it completely wrong: I had purchased the first fire extinguisher I saw. She would have found one that matched the appliances. Worse yet, I paid RP—Retail Price.

Maybe some women pay RP. But I've never met one. Nor am I aware of a store catering to women that actually charges RP.

At department stores like Macy's and Lord & Taylor, everything's always marked down at least once, usually twice. Plus, they send my wife coupons that entitle her to an extra 15 percent off whatever she buys using her store charge card.

She finds an item marked down 40 percent and, for that one day, an additional 25 percent. Her coupon knocks another 15 percent off. A $100 sweater costs just $20 that way.

"Look what I found," she announced proudly the other day, pulling a garment out of a Filene's box. "Pure cashmere. Regularly $499, just $17.95 during Customer Appreciation Days with my coupon."

"It's a man's topcoat, size 56L," I said, examining the tag. "I'm a 40 Regular."

"Maybe you'll grow into it," she said hopefully.

"I haven't grown since 1967."

"No problem, I'll take it back."

And that's another major difference. Women buy things they have no intention of keeping. Retailers allow them do this assuming that a certain percentage will lose their receipts so they'll be unable to return the items.

My wife recently bragged about returning a blouse to T.J. Maxx, a store she says has the most liberal return policy of all. She had purchased it in 1998. A millennium ago.

Saturday I said I was going to Home Depot. "Would you mind returning these throw pillows to Home Goods?" my wife asked. "They're the wrong color."

"So why did you buy them?"

"I thought they might work."

"Our sofa's blue. These are orange. What's Home Goods?"

"It's a store next door to Home Depot. It'll only take a minute."

"Why can't you do it?"

"I need to go Christmas shopping."

So I said yes.

A woman was waiting behind me in the return line at Home Goods when a friend came up to her, held out her hand as if it contained gold dust, and opened a velvet box which revealed a crystal rectangle approximately one by one and a half inches.

"It's just $44.95," she told her friend, her voice trembling with excitement. "Regularly $110."

"What is it?" the friend asked.

"I dunno, but it's Waterford. And they have another one. Think I should buy that one too, before someone else does?"

"It is beautiful. What do you think it is?"

"It's not jewelry. It's too small to be a paperweight. I'm not sure."

"I'd get it if I were you," I interjected.

"Really?"

"Definitely. It's Waterford."

She bought them both.

Bet my bottom dollar she's returned them by now, but that's OK.

That way she won't be depriving another woman of the pleasure of buying them.

Plastic surgery gone awry

Last week I went to meet with a client I hadn't seen for a long time—a woman about my age.

As I was waiting in the lobby the receptionist asked, "Have you seen Colleen lately?"

"No," I replied. "I haven't been here in six months."

"Well you're in for a special treat," she said with a wicked grin.

When Colleen came out to meet me, I saw what she was talking about.

Colleen looked...different. Not totally different, I would have known her anywhere. But her eyes were open wide, giving her a surprised look as if someone had just goosed her. Her smile was as broad as Jack Nicholson's when he played the Joker in *Batman*, and was no longer aligned with her teeth. Most bizarre of all, her head appeared to have been removed then screwed back onto her neck at a 45-degree angle to her body.

When she turned her back and I started to follow her down the hall, the receptionist winked at me, placed both hands on her cheeks and pulled back hard, indicating facelift.

Cosmetic surgery these days is becoming as common as SUVs among aging boomers who, despite personal trainers, swigging gallons of water daily and years of self-imposed starvation, are learning that Newton's law of gravity applies even to them.

Unfortunately there are no guarantees it will achieve the desired results.

Considering a nip, tuck or vacuum-suck yourself? Before you commit, check out www.awfulplasticsurgery.com, a web site that features "before" and "after" shots of celebrities whose procedures didn't exactly turn out the way they might have hoped, and you just might reconsider.

You'll see, for instance, pre- and post-op photos of Marie Osmond, the clean-cut, chubby-cheeked cherub who used to sing with her brother Donny.

Now in her late forties, Marie has done some changin', some re-arrangin'. Thanks to a face lift gone awry, she's a dead ringer for Cruella DeVille.

Then there's Priscilla Presley, whom I once ran into while on safari in South Africa's Kruger National Park. (She was in a Land Rover that pulled up alongside the one in which I was a passenger. While everyone else was watching a leopard kill and devour a gazelle, my binoculars were focused on Priscilla—a much more captivating sight.)

Priscilla is now sporting cheek implants that make her look like Alvin the Chipmunk.

Melanie Griffith, Meg Ryan, and Cher have had lip implants that make them appear as if they've just been beaten soundly.

Breast implants I understand and, in fact, applaud. But fat lips? Who wants to kiss someone who looks like that?

Farrah Fawcett, who had the ultimate face, has had so

much work done that she now looks more like Joan Crawford than her former Charlie's Angel self.

The most entertaining shots of all are of Jocelyn Wildenstein, a celebrity only because she's had so much plastic surgery that she now looks more like a cat than a human.

Lest you think I'm picking on women, Al Pacino's eyebrows are a good half-inch higher than they were when he raised them at his brother Fredo in *The Godfather*.

Don Johnson has a new nose that doesn't look that much different from his last two, which are also shown.

The skin on Burt Reynolds' face has been nipped, tucked and stretched so tightly he now resembles Charlie Chan.

Olympic Decathlon gold medalist Bruce Jenner, who has reportedly undergone a nose job, cheek implants, chin implant and several face lifts, looks like a figure from Madame Tussaud's Wax Museum.

When you think about it, it's downright amazing how vain and superficial people can be. It's not enough that these celebrities struck the lucky gene pool in the first place and inherited faces ordinary mortals would kill for, they want to hold on to those faces until their dying day—something that simply isn't possible.

All would do well to remember that it's not what you wear on your face but what's in your heart that's important.

As a celebrity columnist who always needs to look his best, I'm often asked if I would ever consider plastic surgery and my answer is always the same.

Maybe when I turn 50 in ten years or so.

But not before.

The divine Honest Abe

Nothing is sacred any more.
Not even the memory of Honest Abe.
A controversial new book by historian C.A. Tripp entitled *The Intimate World of Abraham Lincoln* makes a strong case that our sixteenth and perhaps most revered president was gay.

Tripp cites as evidence the fact that when Mary Todd Lincoln—whom Abe didn't really like all that much in the first place—was out of town on her fabled New York shopping sprees, Abe would invite David Derickson, captain of his bodyguard company, over for pajama parties during which Derickson wore Abe's nightshirt and they shared a bed.

He also references a poem romanticizing same-sex marriage Abe wrote as a young man, and describes years of risque correspondence between Lincoln and his lifelong friend and bunkmate, Joshua Speed.

Was Lincoln, the founder of the Republican party, gay?

Nobody knows for sure. But here are excerpts from an unsigned diary my mother purchased in a Springfield, Ill., antique shop 50 years ago, which she dug out and sent me after she saw a TV report about Tripp's book.

If Abe isn't the author, who is?
Judge for yourself.

February 27, 1860
Gave rousing campaign speech today at Cooper Union in New York that had the crowd yelling for more. Afterwards ducked into East Village for cocktails and intimate dinner with Josh. Feeling giddy after two Cosmopolitans, we stopped in piercing parlor and had left ears pierced as symbols of everlasting friendship.

March 4, 1861
Inauguration Day! Was 20 minutes late—couldn't decide whether to wear DKNY or Ralph to the big event. Finally decided to wear something Calvin had whipped up for me. Was unable to hold back tears when Chicago Gay Men's Chorus performed *Battle Hymn of the Republic.* "Oh mine eyes have seen the glory of the coming of the Lord" indeed! Tonight attended series of gala balls. Wore Armani.

April 14, 1861
Damn! Confederates fired on boys at Ft. Sumter. I'm so furious at Jefferson Davis that I swear I would like nothing more than to bitch-slap some sense into him and his red-state minions.

June 11, 1862
Cute intern waved hi as he walked by the Oval Office. I invited him in and told him to have a seat. I asked why he wanted to work in the White House. His answer, delivered with an adorable smile: "Because I've always wanted to play with Lincoln Logs." I told him

that was a good answer, shut the door and asked my secretary, Mrs. Kennedy, to cancel all appointments.

January 4, 1863
Amazing. News media seems to have misinterpreted the Emancipation Proclamation I issued three days ago, and is reporting that I intended to free the *slaves!* Maybe I should have called it the Liberation Proclamation???

November 19, 1863
Gave speech today in Gettysburg. Would have talked longer than two minutes but by the time the crowd had listened to Edward Everett drone on and on for two hours, I was beside myself to get back to D.C. because the decorator, finally, was ready to present his sketches for living quarters. Loved the taffeta swatches for the drapes. Loathed his choice in rugs. Finally had to put my foot down and tell him to go to ABC Carpet in NYC and ask for Pierre.

December 22, 1863
Posed for official portrait today. Artist kept telling me to face front and center but I insisted on turning to the left. With re-election coming up next year, I don't want voters to see my pierced ear. Might be a major turn-off for voters in conservative states like Ohio and Indiana!

April 9, 1865
From Appomattox comes word that Lee has "surrendered" to Grant. How romantic! Though I always had my suspicions about REL, I had no idea Ulysses was "one of the boys." Must invite David over to celebrate.

April 14, 1865
MT and I are going to Ford's Theater tonight to see "Our American Cousin." Now that war has ended, I must get out more. Absolutely adore the theater.

A double date with Trista and Ryan

I'm in the advertising business.

Have been since 1975, but lately I've been thinking of doing something that makes more sense—like volunteering to go door-to-door for Ralph Nader's campaign—because, try as I might, I don't understand a lot of the advertising I'm seeing these days.

To wit, the latest issue of *Promo*, a trade magazine, features the following story: "The sexual lubricant brand K-Y® is getting romantic, encouraging couples around the country to go on dates via a sweepstakes that awards a double date with *The Bachelorette* duo Trista and Ryan Sutter."

Having been hoping for the chance to go on a double date with publicity whores Trista and Ryan, who got married after falling in love on ABC's highly-rated reality show, I logged on to www.k-y.com. There I learned that the grand prize included round-trip air for two to Los Angeles and two nights' stay at an "exclusive" hotel from which winners will be escorted to an "undisclosed location" for their double date.

A press release announced that the promotion was in honor of "National Date Night" for which couples were being encouraged to "Save The Date" and, I assume, to load up with K-Y®. It also included quotes from a sexpert named (I'm not making this up) Michele Weiner-Davis, who gushed, "National Date Night is about...setting aside private time to relax and have fun with your partner."

I also learned, in the Q and A section of the site, the answer to something I've been wondering about for years — the origins of the brand name K-Y. "Two popular myths are that it was created in Kentucky, hence 'K-Y,' or that the letters represent the key ingredients used to make the lubricant. Neither of these is true. The name continues to remain a bit of a mystery."

As does the reason any marketing director with half a brain would approve such a cockamamie promotion. Perhaps he or she was lubricated when the agency presented it.

OK, I recognize that K-Y® probably isn't the easiest product for an MBA to promote. Professors don't teach case studies about lubricant.

And I'm not claiming that everything my agency has created over the years has been in the best of taste, either.

We once pitched a condom marketer on the idea of creating a catalog of free gifts for frequent users that included a string of Christmas lights in the shape of multi-colored foil condom packages. The brand's promotion manager rejected the idea and said he'd rather insert coupons for savings on Subway sandwiches into specially-marked packages.

He showed us the door when we asked if he wanted coupons for six- or twelve-inch Subways.

It's just that I can't imagine anyone being stimulated (a marketing term) to purchase a specific brand of anything—hamburgers, cars, staplers or sexual lubricant—for the chance to win a double date with Trista and Ryan.

Nor can I imagine how the winner broke the news to his or her "date."

Winner: "Honey, do we have plans for Friday?"
Date: "No."
Winner: "We do now. I entered a K-Y sexual lubricant sweepstakes and won a trip."
Date: "Oh, I've been wondering why we suddenly have 20 bottles of that stuff on our bedside table."
Winner: "Yeah, I needed proofs of purchase to enter. Anyway, we're flying to LA to go on a double date at an undisclosed location with Trista and Ryan of *The Bachelorette*."
Date: "What do you mean, an undisclosed location? Why won't they tell you where they're taking us?"
Winner: "Maybe it's because they're afraid Trista and Ryan will be mobbed by their adoring fans if they announce in advance where they will be appearing."
Date: "Oh my God, what are we going to tell people? What if this gets out?"
Winner: "Uh…the PR people from Johnson & Johnson are sending a photographer who's on his way here right now to take our picture. They're gonna distribute it with a press release to the national media."
Date (bursting into tears if a woman, smashing his fist through the wall if a man): "How could you?"
Winner: "Come here baby, let me make it up to you."
Date: "DON'T YOU TOUCH ME."

One piece of bad news though. It's too late to enter; the sweepstakes is over.

But hey, there's always next year.

Save the date.

A shorts story

As we were getting dressed the other morning, my wife pointed out that my undershorts no longer serve the purpose for which they were engineered—namely, to keep her from dying of humiliation if I'm ever rushed to the hospital and the E.R. staff has to cut my clothes off, leaving me lying naked on a gurney but for shorts that look as though they were used to polish brass before someone threw them in the trash.

"That's ludicrous," I replied. "A doctor would never say, 'Mrs. Dryden, your husband is in grave condition, but since you let him out of the house wearing the most revolting underwear I've personally ever seen on a human being, including underwear I saw the year I served in the Peace Corps in Bangladesh, I'm going to let him die to teach you a lesson.'"

"Look in the mirror," she said. "The elastic is shot, there are holes everywhere and they're the color of yellow wax build-up. It's disgusting, and all your shorts are equally gross. If you got hit by a bus, I'd be so embarrassed."

Well not as embarrassed as I'd be. You have to be an idiot to get hit by a bus.

I've only known one, and that was in Auxvasse, Mo.

where I grew up. Her name was Fairy McAfee, a skittish, skinny high school music teacher in her fifties who always wore a straw hat with ribbons. Only one bus a day passed through town, and it stopped every morning at 9:45 at the J&J Café.

Fairy, who never learned to drive, used to ride the bus to Jefferson City every Saturday to visit her son, Skeeter, who was serving time in the State Penitentiary for torching his mother's place of employment. She should have known the routine well. The bus always stopped at the one flashing red light in town, then continued half a block in first gear, before pulling up in front of the J&J.

For some reason that hot summer day, Fairy, seeing the bus coming down the street, decided it wasn't going to stop and ran toward it like a crazed deer charging a car, waving her arms, screaming, "Stop! Stop!"

The driver, who was swigging an R.C. Cola at that precise moment, didn't see her.

Fairy was flattened like a pancake, straw hat and all.

But I digress.

"So go out this weekend and buy new underwear," my wife ordered. "New jeans and shirts, too. I'm sick of seeing you in the same clothes every day, just because you hate to shop."

She knows me well. I hate shopping more than anything—especially clothes shopping.

I used to be quite the clotheshorse 20 years ago. Of course, that was B.C. (before children) when we lived in Manhattan. Back then I worked out daily, had a 31-inch waist, 43-inch chest and clothes-shopped every weekend. My underwear was always pristine. My wife took a picture of me wearing nothing but skivvies on the balcony of an Athens hotel, as I postured like a Greek god, the Parthenon in the background.

Now that I'm past 50 my measurements are reversed and I no longer care about clothes. What's the point? I'll just outgrow them anyway. Whether I shop in the Polo department at Bloomingdale's or at Wal-Mart, there's no way I'll ever look god-like again.

The last place I bought clothing was in the meat department of a local supermarket where, last winter for some reason, there was a table of cashmere sweaters from Madagascar for $39. I bought a blue one. I've worn it every day for two weeks, with the same pair of frayed Eddie Bauer jeans.

I'm writing this on a Saturday afternoon in my office. My wife thinks I'm out buying new undershorts. She'll be annoyed when I come home empty-handed and tell her I was so overwhelmed by having to choose between BVD, Jockey and Hanes that I couldn't decide.

Big deal. I know she'll buy the shorts for my birthday. She always does.

In the meantime, if you run over me with a bus or your Suburban, do her a favor.

Try to restrain yourself and let the E.R. people cut my clothes off, OK?

Parents' Weekend

My wife and I just returned from attending Parents' Weekend at the University of Colorado in Boulder where our youngest son is a freshman.

The highlight was a football game between the Colorado Buffaloes and Iowa State Cyclones played at Folsom Field, which has to be the most beautifully situated college stadium in the country, overlooking the Flatirons of the Rockies.

A C.U. sophomore kicked a 60-yard field goal—a school record—then, for good measure, followed up with a 54-yard field goal.

C.U. won 19-14.

Some random observations about the weekend:

Boys and their toys: My son wanted to take his TV to college. I refused. "You're not going there to be entertained, you're going to study," I told him firmly.

You can imagine how delighted I was to walk into his dorm room and find that his roommate had brought a $3,000 big-screen plasma TV and Sony X-Box.

Campus Crusaders For Christ are as crazy as ever: When I was in college, the wildest guy in my fraternity discovered Jesus one day while tripping on acid, joined the Campus Crusade for Christ, renounced his wicked ways and started preaching from atop a soapbox on the busiest street corner in Columbia, Mo.

Shortly thereafter, he quit college to take his message on the road.

Spectators trekking toward the Colorado stadium last weekend had to pass a California surfer-type blonde who was holding aloft a six-foot banner that read, "Love Jesus or Burn in Hell," a phrase she was also screaming at the top of her lungs, though nobody was paying her any attention.

We were looking for the Microbiolology Building where we were to meet our son.

"Excuse me," I said, tapping her on the shoulder. "Do you know where Microbiology is?"

She ignored me and continued screaming.

Too bad. She had the opportunity to help the two lost souls in the crowd who would have actually have listened to her and blew it.

Twirlers are history: My wife, who was the University of Missouri Golden Girl—the baton twirler in a skimpy gold sequined suit who was always the featured attraction during halftime shows—was shocked to see that C.U. has no baton twirlers, only girls wearing long pants and jackets who twirl huge flags slowly. (Perhaps the baton twirlers were burning in hell for showing too much leg.)

"It's the dumbing down of twirling," she observed disapprovingly. "In my day, twirlers were twirlers."

Buffalo burgers, anyone?: Colorado's mascot is Ralphie, a live buffalo who leads the team onto the field, and is then run around the perimeter of the stadium by college boys in cowboy outfits, and into a trailer attached to a pick-up which immediately speeds off.

It was disturbing to see Ralphie disappear into the trailer because it has a logo on the side announcing that it is provided courtesy of Outback Steak House.

Proof positive jocks are dum: C.U. had one field goal and one touchdown called back, and was penalized two additional times, for having too many players on the field.

Once I can understand but four times in one game?

You can take a boy to college but you still can't take him shopping: While our son was in class Friday afternoon, my wife and I went to the local Nordstrom's. In the men's department I saw a boy in a C.U. sweatshirt following his parents who were carrying sweaters, boxes of shoes, slacks and other wearables.

"I don't want all this stuff, why are you buying it?" the boy wailed.

"Because you need it whether you know it or not," his mother snapped.

Pom-pom girls have evolved: All 12 girls on C.U.'s pom-pom squad wore midriff-exposing outfits that revealed perfectly flat abs, a term nobody had heard of when I was in college. Judging from CU's squad, a flat abdomen is the most important criterion a candidate must have if she wants to be a pom-pom girl (and I trust my feminist readers will forgive me for calling them "girls." Somehow "pom-pom women" doesn't sound right).

When I was in college, pom-pom girls needed something only one of the CU girls appeared to have—big pom-poms.

The halftime show is still for old farts: C.U.'s halftime show was entitled "A Salute to the Beatles," an obvious attempt to pander to the parents in attendance.

And for one brief moment it worked. I felt like I was back in college again.

Until I got up to go to the men's room and caught sight in the mirror of a gray-haired guy with a "Parent's Weekend" name tag on his sweater.

That shook me up, let me tell you.

You have 14 messages

Used to be that when you arrived home after a long weekend away, you could stay in vacation mode for a few days until you caught up with everything that had happened in your absence.

Today, thanks to your telephone answering machine, you find out instantly.

Within moments after walking through the door, you're as stressed as when you left.

My wife and I went out of town one recent weekend. Here's what we found on our answering machine when we returned.

8:21 p.m. Friday—This is Mike at Triple C Septic Service. Sorry I missed our appointment this afternoon, I got stuck on a job in Greenwich. Whaddya say we make it Monday at 4? If I don't hear from you, I'll assume that's fine, OK? See ya then.

8:22 p.m. Friday—Mike at Triple C again. My wife reminds me I have to baby-sit the kids Monday afternoon—she's getting her roots done —so let's make it 4 o'clock Tuesday. Call if that's a problem, otherwise ... see ya then.

9:44 a.m. Saturday—Hello, my name is Takesha. I'm calling from the University of Missouri to invite New

York area alumni to cocktails and dinner Tuesday Nov. 11 in Manhattan with Coach Quinn Snyder who will be providing an insider preview of this year's Tiger basketball team. The cost is $500 per couple to benefit the new sports complex building fund. If you're interested, please call me back at ...

9:53 a.m. Saturday—Hi Mr. And Mrs. Dryden, this is Shelby at the dog kennel. I know you like your dachshunds to board together in the same stall but Bonnie is eating Clyde's poopies so we're going to move her to a private one. If you get this message and don't want us to separate them please call...

11:50 a.m. Saturday—Hey, it's Mike at Triple C. My son's birthday is Tuesday and we're having 10 five-year-olds over, so the earliest I can come out to look at that back-up is...uh...December 5th at 2 p.m. Hope that's convenient. See ya then.

3:31 p.m. Saturday—These ees Jesus I pant your hose tree years ago and am wandering eef you wont me to pant sam more mebe a leetle touch-up iran de treem or mebe eensod work if you do plez coll me at ...

5:55 p.m. Saturday—Ohmigod! I'm in front of your house and there's a coyote strolling up your sidewalk as if he owns the place! For Godsakes don't step outside, I think he's foaming at the mouth! Ohmigod!

6:30 p.m. Saturday—This is Home Security. We just received a signal from your attic fire alarm. If you don't call back in two minutes we'll call the Fire Department and have them dispatch a truck.

3:13 a.m. Sunday—Marvin? Are you there? Pick up Marvin or, I swear, I'm going to call the cops and have you hauled off to jail once and for all you sick, perverted son-of-a ... Oh wait, I meant to call area code 213.

Never mind.

10 a.m. Sunday—Hi Tom, this is Ross Smith at Cosmopolitan Life. It's been 19 years since I wrote your term life policy and, as I do every three months, I'm calling to see if perhaps your needs have changed. I'll call back tomorrow. Stay well.

11:31 a.m. Sunday—Mike at Triple C. I'll be in your neighborhood tomorrow after all and maybe I can stop by and take a quick look-see after all. I'll probably be there with a crew oh, sometime between 10 and 4. Call me back to confirm. See ya then.

2:25 p.m. Sunday—This is Northworst Airways calling to let you know your return flight to LaGuardia this evening has been canceled. For your convenience, we've re-booked you on flight 134 leaving this afternoon at 3:30. Please plan to arrive at the airport at least one hour before departure ... and thank you for flying Northworst.

4:45 p.m. Sunday—Mom? Dad? Don't flip out or anything but I'm in the infirmary. Call me on my cell, OK? If I don't answer I might be in surgery. Love you ...

7:44 p.m. Sunday—This is Mike at Triple C. How come you didn't have the common courtesy to return my call after I went to the trouble of re-arranging my schedule? If I don't hear from you tonight I'm going to assume you've made arrangements with some other septic company and I certainly hope you treat them with more respect than you treated me ...

Trust in the Lard

I was telling my family recently about the incredible cookies my 91-year-old mother, Ruby, used to bake to take to church ice cream socials when I was a boy in Auxvasse, Mo.

She called them "Icebox Cookies."

Ruby mixed the dough in a bowl, rolled it into logs she wrapped in wax paper, and stuck the logs in the fridge to chill. Then she sliced the dough and baked the cookies.

I started salivating as I described the taste, so I called Ruby for the recipe.

"First you take a cup of lard…" she said.

"Lard?"

"You know what lard is!" she said, sounding hurt as if she had caught me trying to deny my deep-fried culinary heritage.

"Of course I know. It's rendered pig fat. I bet grocery stores don't even sell it any more."

"Well, I suppose you could substitute butter but they won't taste as good."

That night, I made Ruby's Icebox Cookies using butter.

They couldn't hold a candle to the cookies I remember.

Ruby, as good cooks always are, was right. For some things there are no substitutes. Of course, back in the fifties when she was feeding her family chicken-fried steak (in lard, of course) smothered with white gravy, along with vegetables seasoned with jowl (another form of animal fat favored by southern cooks), nobody had heard of cholesterol.

Little wonder millions of boomers raised on country cooking have stratospheric cholesterol levels today and why, in my youth, so many Auxvasse people suffered fatal heart attacks at relatively young ages. The phone would ring and we would hear Ruby murmuring "I'm so sorry" into the receiver. She would hang up and announce sadly, "So and so just dropped dead."

We'd shrug our shoulders, and reach for another lard-laced cookie. Who would have guessed?

I found myself reminiscing about lard and other artery-clogging foods of my youth the other day as I wandered through a supermarket that specializes in "healthy" (e.g. "fake") foods.

In the bakery were brownies made not with sugar and chocolate but with honey and carob.

Baked veggie sticks were on sale in the snack food section.

The deli featured salad bowls full of sesame-covered tofu chunks.

After admiring the polished organic fruit and sampling the goat cheese and garbanzo-bean curry (vomitorious), I picked up a few items and headed for the checkout line.

An anorexic-thin woman in black tights was unloading a cartful of pretend food onto the belt. A pint of an imitation ice cream called "Rice Cream." Sugar-free, chocolate-free "baking chips." Soy butter. Organic decaf coffee. And bottle after bottle of water—organic no doubt—as if she was planning a trek across the Sahara rather than driving home in her SUV (a fake truck) to treat her kids to cookies made with chocolate-free chips and bowls of cream-free Rice Cream.

On my way home, I swung by an ethnic supermarket where, to my amazement, I found lard.

I bought it and made a batch of Ruby's Icebox Cookies.

Because they contained roughly as much fat per cookie as a half-pound of fried bacon, nobody else in the family (other than our dachshunds who will eat anything) would touch them.

They tasted exactly as they should but something was still missing—homemade vanilla ice cream.

Remembering the old-fashioned ice cream churner I bought at a garage sale for $1.50 that has sat in a dark corner of the basement for 15 years, I called Ruby for her recipe.

"First you stir your egg yolks into your heavy cream…" she said.

"Egg yolks? Cream?"

Lard have mercy.

Ruby's Icebox Cookies

1 C lard (OK, butter if you must, but don't even think about using margarine)
2 C light brown sugar
3 1/2 C flour
1 tsp baking soda
2 eggs
1/2 C chopped pecans

Mix well, form into several rolls, wrap in waxed paper, and place in icebox until firm. Slice and bake at 350 degrees for 10 minutes. Enjoy with a cold glass of 100 percent whole milk (as long as you're mainlining fat, you might as well forget skim or one percent) and two Lipitor or other cholesterol-inhibiting drugs of your choice.

A day by the bay

To celebrate his 22nd birthday, my wife and I last Sunday took our son to the epicenter of America's drug culture. Then we spent the afternoon drinking.

All in the name of furthering his education, of course.

We were in San Francisco visiting nearby law schools our son is interested in attending. While Scott McKenzie in his one (and only) hit of the sixties urged those who go to San Francisco to "be sure and wear some flowers in your hair," we weren't wearing flowers.

We were wearing hair gel, having awoken to find our hotel near Union Square was without hot water due, the front desk staff claimed, to a failure of the underground steam system that powered its boilers.

Unwilling to shower in ice water, we slicked back our bed-heads and off we went.

We started our day visiting Haight-Ashbury, which our son had studied in his sixties culture class at Michigan.

I was glad he wanted to see it because I had never been to "the Haight." As a teenager, I had often pictured myself walking through it wearing bell bottoms and sandals with hair down to my shoulders (sans gel, of course, which hadn't been invented) headed to a love-in or, at the very least, to hear the Jefferson Airplane or Cream at the Fillmore.

By the time I finally arrived I was a 53-year-old suburbanite driving a Cadillac Sedan DeVille (upgrade compliments of Avis) equipped with XM satellite radio tuned to a sixties station.

In what had to be karma, McKenzie's song came on just as we reached Buena Vista Park.

McKenzie promised we would meet some gentle people there but we didn't. It's hard to meet anyone when you're cruising through a neighborhood in a car the size of a Sherman tank.

If I wasn't what Haight-Asbury was expecting a child of the sixties to be, the intersection of Haight and Ashbury wasn't what I was expecting either.

On one corner was a Ben & Jerry's, a subsidiary of Unilever. (The thought that the company's best-selling flavor worldwide is named after the district's most famous one-time resident, a man who is now dead and probably none too grateful about it, was heavy, man.)

On the opposite corner was a GAP.

We might as well have been in Westport, Conn.

We did, however, see a vintage pumpkin-yellow Volkswagen bus parked on the street. A "D.A.R.E. to Keep Your Kid Off Drugs" sticker was affixed to the bumper.

Far out.

Having seen all there was to see, we crossed the Golden Gate bridge to Marin County, then wended our way around the bay to the Napa Valley where, I had announced, we would find a winery that sold bread, cheese and salami and have ourselves a nice picnic lunch with a bottle of wine.

But we took a wrong turn and got lost.

By the time we finally arrived in Yountville, we were starving. I pulled the Caddy into the parking lot of the first restaurant we saw which—we soon learned to our dismay—was A.) ridiculously expensive and B.) French, which meant the menu featured salads made with weeds I pay a lawn service to kill, frogs' legs, blood sausage, braised rabbit and other repulsive dishes Americans make a pretense of having difficulty choosing between while silently praying the waiter will suddenly remember that the special of the day is a QP Cheese *avec pommes frites*.

Once the menu had been presented it was too late to walk out—we had already devoured the crusty baguette and tub of butter our waiter, Philippe, had sat before us, so we had to order.

Having dropped somewhere north of $125 on an unsatisfying lunch, we continued up the road, stopping at the Mondavi, Beringer and BV wineries.

At each we tasted a flight of five wines, listening solemnly and pretending to care deeply as employees pointed out scents and tastes that made each unique, including undertones of fresh-mown hay, figs, chocolate, tobacco and—my favorite—gravel.

Late in the afternoon we headed back to San Francisco. As the last pink-orange streaks of the day faded over the Bay, we arrived at the University of California-Berkeley where, judging by the restaurants surrounding the campus, nine out of ten students apparently subsist on Indian vegan cuisine.

Groovier than frogs' legs or rabbit I suppose.

But not by much.

How I'll spend eternity

If, when I die, I go to hell, I know exactly what my punishment will be.

I'll spend eternity in a football field-sized home improvement superstore, where I'll be forced to wander the aisles looking for merchandise I wouldn't recognize if it were in front of me, begging assistance from clerks who speak gobbledygook.

On days the devil is in a particularly sadistic mood, I'll also have to dodge forklift trucks whose drivers will sneak up behind me and beep their horns, making me leap straight into the air.

Come to think of it, that's how I've spent my free time for the last six months ever since we decided to have our master bathroom remodeled.

A friend last fall introduced me to a Latvian contractor who quoted a great price for renovating the bathroom which my wife claimed was looking "tired." (It looked fine to me. Everything worked.)

Once the custom-order cabinets arrived, the entire project, we were assured, would take a week.

He said the work would go faster if, on my way home from work, I would stop at a major home improvement superstore to pick up materials as he needed them.

I thought it would be easy. Dumb me.

Some men, you see, can zip in and out of home improvement stores in seconds, finding exactly what they're looking for. These are the guys who, while standing in the checkout line, boast to each other about their tools or whatever it is handy men talk about when they get together. (I overheard one guy bragging about how easy it was for him to locate studs. Amazing how brazen people are these days.)

I, on the other hand, was born without the part of my brain that, if I had it, would enable me to understand how things work or go together.

A home improvement superstore is my worst nightmare because I'm clueless as to what I'm looking for or what department it's in.

For example, one night the contractor faxed me a list that began with, "Ten drywall screws."

I drove to the store and started roaming the aisles.

After a half hour I asked a clerk for help.

"You want fine or rough screws?" he asked.

"Uh, fine," I answered. (All the bathroom décor books say the room should be a soothing sanctuary from the stresses of daily life. So nothing rough.)

"Number eight or six?"

"What's the difference?"

"One's eight, one's six."

"Gimme six." (It's one of my lucky roulette numbers.)

"You want one, one and a quarter, two or three inchers?"

"What do you recommend?"

"Are you using regular or Type X drywall?"

"Beats me. It's a bathroom."

"I'd guess Type X."
"So what's right for Type X?"
"Depends how thick it is."
"Just give me 10 of everything."
"Metal or plastic?"
"What would you buy?"
"Metal is better."
"My sentiments exactly."
Total elapsed time: 48 minutes.

The next item on my list was "wall switch."

I never knew they came in so many varieties. Single pole. Double pole. 15-amp. 20-amp.

I bought one of each. That took another hour.

A few days later, after our special order Ice Grey Kohler elongated toilet which, the brochure promises, "delivers robust flushing power," had been delivered, I was dispatched to the store for a ballcock kit.

I was too embarrassed to ask for help finding that. Once I located them, I bought eight.

None worked.

This went on for months with a six-week hiatus during which the contractor vanished. (We later learned he had been on vacation in Latvia.)

But, at long last, the bathroom is almost finished, once the custom drop-in sinks which have been back-ordered since October arrive.

Now I have to return all the stuff the contractor didn't use. I've saved receipts and have over $1,000 worth of hardware, plumbing supplies and electrical thingies stashed in the trunk of my car.

But maybe I'll keep them.

He starts work on the guest bathroom next week.

Hogging the phone

The *Chicago Tribune* reports that a number of new parents who apparently possess the collective IQs of a brick of Philadelphia Cream Cheese are naming their children after status brands.

According to the Social Security Administration, of the four million babies born in 2000, there were six Timberlands, 298 Armanis, 25 Infinitis, 21 L'Oreals and, my favorite, seven Courvoisiers.

Unfortunate names to be sure, but I've heard worse.

For example, my father-in-law had an aunt Iva Estes who, years before it was acceptable for women to keep their maiden names, married a man named Payne.

Iva got off lucky compared to legendary Texas philanthropist and arts patroness, Ima Hogg.

Having heard of Miss Hogg but knowing nothing about her, I went to google.com and did a search. Here's what I learned. (The comments in parentheses are mine alone for which I will no doubt be repaid by someday having a grandchild named Lexus.)

HOGG, IMA (1882-1975) daughter of Governor James Hogg, was born in Mineola, Texas, and was known as Miss Ima. *(She never married for obvious reasons. Suitors were few and far between.)* In 1917 she helped found the Houston Symphony Society and, in 1940, having suffered a breakdown *(lots of kids blame their problems on their parents but in Ima's case it was justified)*, established the Hogg Foundation for Mental Hygiene. In 1943 Ima Hogg was elected to the Houston school board *(after which kids complained more than ever about the slop in the cafeteria).* In 1969, the town of Quitman established the Ima Hogg Museum in her honor *(they wanted to call it the Petunia Pig Museum but lawyers for Warner Brothers objected).* In 1972 she received the Thomas Jefferson Award for outstanding contributions to America's cultural heritage *(having somehow survived living with the worst name in American history).* She is buried in the Hogg family plot in Austin *(next to her brother Whatta).* The beneficiary of her will was the Ima Hogg Foundation established in 1964 *(which sure as hell will never award a grant to Tom Dryden).*

Wanting to learn more, I called long distance information to get the number of the Ima Hogg Museum.

In the old days before Jim-muh Carter busted up AT&T (one more reason they should take his Nobel Peace Prize away), obtaining a number from a long distance operator was easy; the operator lived in the area you were calling and was therefore familiar with it.

Now you get a computer voice that asks, "What city?" ("Quitman," I said), "What state? ("Texas") and "What listing? ("The Ima Hogg Museum").

A moment later an operator, sounding heavily medicated and who could have been in Indiana or India but certainly not in Texas judging from her accent, came on the line.

"How are you spelling that?"

"H-o-g-g."

"And what's the first name?
"Ima, spelled i-m-a.
"Did you say 'Ima Hogg?'"
"Don't be so hard on yourself, you sound like a lovely person."
Silence.
"I want the Ima Hogg Museum."
"I'm sorry, there's no listing."
Click.

That reminded me of a story related by my friend Sonja who, planning a second visit to the FDR Museum in Hyde Park, New York, called 914 information to find out when it was open.

"I'd like the number of the FDR Museum in Hyde Park," Sonja told the operator.

"I'm sorry, I can't find a listing for the FDR Museum."

"Try the Franklin D. Roosevelt Museum."

"There's no Franklin D. Roosevelt Museum either."

"How about the Franklin Delano Roosevelt Museum?"

"No listing, sorry."

"I know it's there, I've been there!"

"Would you like to speak to my supervisor?"

"Yes, please."

When the supervisor came on, Sonja told her, "I want the number of the Franklin Delano Roosevelt Museum."

"Is that a residence or business?"

"Neither one, he was president of the United States and he's *dead*," Sonja shouted into the phone. "Haven't you heard of him?

"No I haven't."

"Where are you anyway?"

"Oregon."

Turned out Sonja had it wrong. It's the Franklin D. Roosevelt Library. A New York operator would have been able to find it.

I can see it now. In 200 years people will be calling operators asking for the "Lexus Versace Dryden Presidential Museum."

May not sound as impressive as the Franklin Delano Roosevelt Museum.

But it beats the Ima Hogg Museum any day of the week.

How about a martini?

I lost a good friend the other day.

His name was Ed but those of us in his SAE pledge class at the University of Missouri in the fall of 1970 called him Egg. He was one of the few friends from my youth I made a point of staying in touch with.

Though Egg grew up in a distinguished Kansas City family, he was the most down-to-earth guy you could ever hope to meet.

After college, Egg landed a job at a radio station in an Arkansas delta town an hour up the interstate from Memphis.

To everyone's amazement, Egg never left that sleepy little town in the heart of cotton country. He married local women and became active in regional politics and civic affairs. He even developed an Arkansas accent. At the time of his death, he was partner in a company that owned a chain of radio stations.

Egg committed suicide. Turned a shotgun on himself. Didn't leave a note. Nobody saw it coming.

I learned about it from a message his wife left on our answering machine. His brother Steve, when I called, said he couldn't bear the thought of standing up in front of a funeral home full of people and eulogizing Egg. He said he would be grateful if I would.

So I did.

And I'm glad I did.

I wanted people to remember the guy in the polished wood coffin for his sense of humor—one of the best of anyone I've ever had the privilege of knowing—rather than for his exit strategy.

I wanted to tell funny stories that would make them laugh—the kind he always told. We all needed to laugh.

So I told them how Egg loved to tell about the time a computer glitch caused his pre-programmed gospel station to start broadcasting gangsta rap that was supposed to be playing on the urban station, and vice versa, making the phones ring off the hook.

I told them about the ancient Shelley Berman comedy album he played so often he memorized it. His favorite bit was a sketch about a nervous airline passenger who summoned the stewardess (Berman said the plural was "stewardeye"), mistakenly believing something was wrong with the plane. I imitated Egg imitating Berman:

Passenger: "Uh, miss…the wing is on fire."

Robotic stewardess: "Coffee, tea or milk?"

Passenger, becoming agitated: "We don't have time for coffee tea or milk. We're doomed."

Stewardess, perking up: "Well then, how about a martini?"

I told them about the time I sent Egg a copy of my first book—a compilation of columns written for the local paper. Shortly thereafter John Grisham came to Egg's town to promote his latest book at a local bookstore. While Grisham's back was turned, Egg placed my book atop the stack of books Grisham was signing and took a Polaroid picture. It made it look like people were lined up to get a copy of my self-published book, not Grisham's best-seller, and that Grisham was signing my book, not his.

It was hilarious.

I told them about the SAE Member Directory that had mistakenly listed Egg as deceased, and how he milked that for all it was worth, telling fundraisers who called that he couldn't very well donate to the national chapter because he was dead anyway.

I said I wanted to address Egg directly if he was listening.

I reminded Egg about the only time I could recall that he had ever annoyed me. He had returned from spring break complaining about a poison ivy rash that itched. Turned out he had German measles, which he passed on to half the fraternity, causing us to have to cancel our annual Plantation Ball.

I told Egg that this time he had annoyed me again. In fact, he had annoyed all of us in that room: He had broken our hearts.

Then I told Egg that we forgave him.

And while I had no right to speak for his stricken family or friends, I do forgive him though I can't understand why he did it and never will. Nobody will.

I'm writing this on the plane home from his funeral. In a minute stewardeye will be coming through the cabin with a choice of beverages including complimentary soft drinks, beer and wine for $4 and cocktails for $5, exact change will be appreciated.

Assuming airlines still sell those miniature bottles of premixed cocktails, I believe I'll have a martini tonight.

Maybe two.

A career change

I've been in advertising for 32 years.

I don't know anybody who's had the same job for 32 years.

Lately I've been thinking that maybe I ought to try something new. Something less stressful. So I've been examining my options.

Saturday night, as I was stuffing my face in Little Italy with my wife and her brother, who's from Mississippi, my brother-in-law commented that the only Italian restaurants down there are chain restaurants, like Olive Garden. He said that anyone who opened an authentic Eye-talian eatery in Jackson would make a mint.

I stayed awake half the night considering the possibilities.

I love Italian food. Plus, the cost of living in Mississippi is cheap compared to Connecticut. I can't cook, but that's no problem. A friend who owns an Italian restaurant in New York can make extra sauce, ship it to me, and I can pour it over everything. Mississippians don't know real Italian food, they'll be none the wiser.

On the other hand, I want my nights to be free, so maybe a restaurant isn't such a good idea after all.

So I'll buy an art gallery instead. I found one for sale

on the Internet. It's in Annapolis, Nova Scotia. Just $49,000, including a house with hand-hewn beams. And I already have a collection of 300 vintage posters, a ready-made inventory.

There are, however, a couple of issues.

One, I can't bear the thought of parting with any of my posters. Two, my wife wouldn't want to move to Canada.

Come to think of it, neither would I. It's cold up there in Canada. I hate cold.

But I do like art. Especially African art. I saw two stores in Manhattan selling hand-carved wooden animals from Africa for $100 and up. I recently brought back from South Africa a dozen of the identical carvings for which I paid $2 each. I could have paid less but didn't have the heart to dicker. Rural Africa is so poor it breaks your heart.

Hmmm. If I buy 10,000 carved animals a year for $2 each, build a web site, and charge only $50—half as much as those stores in New York—I can gross $480,000 a year, and help bring prosperity to the Third World. Plus, I can fly back and forth to Africa—my favorite continent—and write off the cost of the trips. Maybe I'll even become an airline pilot so I can fly for free. I'm already taking flying lessons and love it. Granted, two instructors have refused to fly with me any more. But I'm improving with every lesson. And now that I've learned about aerodynamics, I'm getting over my irrational fear that the wings are going to flap off during turbulence. I'm assured that has happened only once in the annals of commercial aviation.

I can hear me now. "Ladies and gentlemen, I've just turned on the seat belt sign because radar is indicating that

THE WINGS ARE ABOUT TO SNAP OFF LIKE TREE LIMBS IN AN ICE STORM AND WE'RE ALL GOING TO DIE. OH, THE HUMANITY!"

I'd surely get fired.

So here's a more practical option.

My wife and I have been taking dancing lessons. I know how to swing, tango, cha-cha, all the dances our parents did in the good old days.

I hear cruise lines hire men to dance with widows who are spending the proceeds of their husbands' life insurance policies. I can read on deck all day and put on my tux every night and play Fred Astaire. Old ladies have always liked me.

But there's no salary. With two sons in college, I need money coming in. Darn, that sounded perfect.

So I'll become a wine importer instead.

I spent a week visiting wineries in South Africa. Virtually unknown to American consumers, South African wines are uniformly excellent and dirt cheap. I can create my own brand, buy in bulk, bottle it here and probably get $20 a bottle. I've already written my first commercial. *"Hi, Nelson Mandela here for Dryden's Cape Country Wines."*

But I can't afford to produce it and buy the network time to air it until I sell my first million cases. A classic Catch 22.

Perhaps I'll take my weekly newspaper column national. My mug can appear in newspapers nationwide, like Dave Barry's and Andy Rooney's. Every year or so I can compile my best columns into a book, pitch it on *Today* and have breakfast afterwards with Katie and Matt.

But no, I read that newspaper revenues are way down. People are getting their news online these days. So there's no demand for print columnists. I'm a dinosaur.

So, I'll write another kind of book. Ralph Nader made a name for himself writing a book about Corvairs, "Unsafe At Any Speed."

I can write one about SUVs and call it "At Least Corvairs Were Cute."

Bet it would sell a million copies.

It's five o'clock. Quitting time. But I'll be back here in the office at my computer tomorrow and, strangely enough, I'm looking forward to it.

You see, I'm bidding on eBay for a scuba rental shop in Costa Rica. It's just three blocks from the beach.

I'll find out at noon tomorrow if it's mine.

A bimbette's story

People magazine is featuring excerpts from "Witness: For the Prosecution of Scott Peterson," a book written by Peterson's massage therapist girlfriend, Amber Frey.

A more fitting title would have been "Witless: A Bimbette Reveals Everything She Knows (Which Isn't Much)."

Because Witless is exactly what Frey and anyone who buys her idiotic sob story is.

Frey provides intimate details about her affair with the fertilizer salesman a jury recently decided should become fertilizer himself once his appeals run out in 20 years or so.

It all started with a blind date a month before Peterson's pregnant wife, Laci, vanished on Christmas Eve.

Moments after meeting, Peterson invited Frey to his hotel room so he could change out of the suit he said he had been wearing all day. (Note to self: Don't forget that it's easier to score with chicks today than it was in your day, so always cut to the chase and ask blind dates to hotel in first five minutes.)

Frey said sure. "It seemed reasonable."

Turned out he hadn't checked into the hotel yet. (Smart move. Why pay for a room unless you're 100 percent sure you're going to need it for something?)

So they registered.

In the elevator going up to the room, he opened a duffel bag, removed two glasses and uncorked a bottle of Champagne.

Emerging from the shower, he remembered something. "He reached into the duffel bag again and pulled out a box of strawberries, and he dropped one in each of our glasses." (Note to self: Remember to take duffel bag containing bubbly and assortment of fruit on next blind date.)

At dinner he told her he lived alone in Sacramento and was "looking forward to settling down but that he hadn't yet found the right person."

Not to mention he hadn't yet found anyone as gullible as Frey.

Finding herself "in no condition to drive home" after an evening of karaoke, she returned with him to the room. They kissed passionately. "I don't know if I'm ready to be with you," she informed him but, like the French army facing the Nazis, she quickly surrendered.

Shortly thereafter, the friend of Frey's who had arranged the blind date learned that Peterson was actually married and living in Modesto.

Peterson told the friend he was sorry he lied and started crying. "It's just—I lost my wife. It's been very hard for me."

A few days later, Peterson confessed to Frey that he had been lying. His wife was alive.

"Feeling confused," a state in which Frey seems to

find herself frequently, she didn't see him again for several days.

But she got over her confusion in time to invite him to a Christmas party the next week where they posed for pictures.

That night she told him she had tried birth control pills in the past "but that they didn't agree with me."

Peterson told her not to worry. He was "thinking" about a vasectomy. So they "were intimate without protection." (Note to self: Always tell dates you're "thinking" about a vasectomy. If they are stupid enough to buy it, you won't have to stop what you're doing, get dressed and run out to the drug store.)

He then informed Frey that, alas, he wouldn't be available over the holidays because he was going duck hunting in Maine.

Christmas morning, as the police were scouring his neighborhood for signs of his missing wife, Peterson called and painted a word picture describing the snow on the trees in Maine.

In honor of his duck-hunting holiday, Frey sang over the phone "Five Little Ducks Went Hunting," the favorite song of her 20-month-old daughter (proof positive birth control pills didn't agree with her).

Finally, four days later, after nonstop news coverage of Laci Peterson's disappearance which Frey didn't recall hearing about because she was so busy celebrating, a friend informed her that her boyfriend's wife was missing and that he was Suspect *Numero Uno*.

Frey called the cops, who urged her to tape her conversations with Peterson.

At the stroke of midnight on New Year's, Peterson called and said he was in Paris on fertilizer business and thinking of her. (Note to self: Always tell girlfriends you're calling from Paris, gazing out the window at the Eiffel Tower. They'll continue to put out in hopes you'll take them along on your next trip.) At that moment, she realized he had been playing her for a sucker. "Of course I knew he wasn't in Europe." (Astonishingly, Frey knew Paris is in Europe.) "But there was still a small part of me (I can guess which part) that missed him or missed the person I thought he was. Only two days earlier I had still been thinking of our future together."

The rest is history. During Peterson's trial, Frey told everything she knew, helping prosecutors nail a guilty verdict.

I could go on and on but I don't have time.

I have a blind date tonight and have to get ready.

Printed in the United States
38510LVS00003B/146